Affiliate Marketing Blueprint

A Comprehensive Guide to Building a Successful Online
Business

Solomon Matthew

DEDICATION

I dedicate this book to the dreamers who refuse to settle for mediocrity, who dare to challenge the status quo, and who believe in their ability to create their own success. You understand that opportunity lies within your grasp, waiting to be seized through strategic thinking, perseverance, and a deep understanding of the affiliate marketing ecosystem.

CONTENTS

Encouragement to take action and implement the affiliate marketing blueprint

Affiliate Marketing Blueprint

ACKNOWLEDGMENTS

I would like to express my deepest gratitude and appreciation to everyone who has contributed to the creation of this book, "Affiliate Marketing Blueprint." Your support, encouragement, and expertise have been invaluable in making this project a reality.

First and foremost, I would like to thank my family for their unwavering support throughout this journey. Your love and understanding have provided me with the motivation and strength to overcome any challenges I faced along the way.

I extend my heartfelt thanks to my friends and colleagues who have provided valuable insights, feedback, and encouragement. Your input and discussions have greatly enriched the content of this book, and I am grateful for the stimulating conversations we have had.

A special thanks to my editor Mr. Joshua, who diligently reviewed and polished the manuscript, offering invaluable suggestions and ensuring the clarity and coherence of the text. Your expertise and attention to detail have been instrumental in shaping the final version of this book.

I would also like to acknowledge the contributions of the

numerous industry experts and affiliate marketers who have generously shared their knowledge and experiences. Your insights have added depth and authenticity to the content, providing readers with practical strategies and techniques to succeed in the world of affiliate marketing.

Lastly, I want to express my sincere appreciation to the readers of this book. Your interest and support are the driving force behind my work. I hope that "Affiliate Marketing Blueprint" proves to be a valuable resource, empowering you to navigate the complex world of affiliate marketing and achieve your goals.

Once again, thank you to all who have contributed to this book. Your involvement has been instrumental in its creation, and I am deeply grateful for your contributions.

Introduction

Affiliate marketing has emerged as a powerful and lucrative way for individuals and businesses to generate income online. The realm of affiliate marketing offers an abundance of opportunities for those willing to learn and implement effective strategies. In the book "Affiliate Marketing Blueprint," readers are taken on a comprehensive journey through the world of affiliate marketing, exploring the principles, techniques, and proven methodologies that can lead to online success.

Affiliate marketing is a popular online business model where individuals or companies (affiliates) promote and sell products or services on behalf of another company (merchant) in exchange for a commission. It is a performance-based marketing strategy that benefits both the affiliates and the merchant.

The affiliate marketing blueprint is the systematic approach or plan that affiliates follow to effectively promote products and generate income. It outlines the key steps and strategies involved in building a successful affiliate marketing business.

Importance of Affiliate Marketing in the Digital Era

In the digital era, affiliate marketing has become increasingly important as a powerful marketing strategy for businesses of all sizes. It has gained significant traction due to its ability to generate results, cost-effectiveness, and its alignment with the evolving nature of online consumer behavior. Affiliate marketing refers to a performance-based marketing model in which businesses reward affiliates for each customer or sale generated through their promotional efforts.

Here are several key reasons why affiliate marketing holds great importance in the digital era:

1. Cost-effective: Affiliate marketing offers a cost-effective approach for businesses to promote their products or services. Unlike traditional advertising methods that often require large upfront investments, affiliate marketing operates on a pay-for-performance basis. Advertisers only pay affiliates when they successfully drive a desired action, such as a sale or lead.

This results in a more efficient allocation of marketing budgets and reduces the risk of wasted ad spend.

2. Increased reach and brand exposure: Through affiliate marketing, businesses can tap into a vast network of affiliates who have their own unique online platforms, such as websites, blogs, social media accounts, and email lists. This enables brands to reach a wider audience and gain exposure to potential customers who may not have been aware of their products or services otherwise. Affiliates act as brand advocates, promoting products to their followers or readership, and driving targeted traffic to the advertiser's website.

3. Performance-based results: One of the key advantages of affiliate marketing is its performance-based nature. Advertisers can set specific goals and metrics they want affiliates to achieve, such as sales, leads, or clicks. Since affiliates are motivated by commissions or incentives, they have a vested interest in driving high-quality traffic and conversions. This results in a more accountable and measurable marketing approach, where advertisers can track the success of their campaigns and optimize accordingly.

4. Builds trust and credibility: Affiliates often have established relationships with their audience, built on trust and credibility. When affiliates recommend a

product or service, their audience is more likely to trust their opinion, leading to higher conversion rates. This trust factor helps businesses enhance their reputation and reach potential customers who may have reservations about purchasing from unfamiliar brands. Affiliate marketing enables advertisers to leverage the trust and influence of affiliates to boost their brand's credibility and reputation.

5. Diversification of marketing channels: In the digital era, consumers interact with brands across various channels and platforms. Affiliate marketing allows businesses to diversify their marketing efforts by leveraging different affiliate partners and their respective platforms. This helps expand the brand's presence and reach across multiple touch points, including websites, blogs, social media, email newsletters, and more. By utilizing different affiliates, businesses can engage with audiences in diverse niches and demographics, maximizing their chances of reaching the right customers.

6. Scalability and flexibility: Affiliate marketing offers scalability and flexibility, making it suitable for businesses of all sizes. It allows advertisers to easily scale their campaigns by recruiting more affiliates and expanding their reach. Additionally, businesses can tailor their affiliate marketing strategies to align with their

specific goals, target audience, and budget. Whether it's partnering with niche influencers or running large affiliate networks, the flexibility of affiliate marketing makes it adaptable to various business needs.

Affiliate marketing plays a crucial role in the digital era by providing businesses with a cost-effective, performance-based, and scalable marketing strategy. It enables brands to extend their reach, tap into new customer segments, and build trust and credibility through trusted affiliate partners. As digital channels continue to evolve, affiliate marketing remains a valuable tool for businesses to drive sales, increase brand exposure, and achieve their marketing objectives.

CHAPTER ONE

Understanding Affiliate Marketing

Affiliate marketing is a performance-based marketing model in which individuals or businesses, known as affiliates, promote products or services offered by another company, called the merchant or advertiser. The affiliate earns a commission or a predetermined reward for each successful referral or sale generated through their marketing efforts.

Here's a comprehensive explanation of how affiliate marketing works:

1. Participants: Affiliate marketing involves three primary participants:

*Merchant/Advertiser: This is the company that owns the product or service being promoted. They offer an affiliate program to attract affiliates who will promote their products.

Affiliate Marketing Blueprint

*Affiliate/Publisher: Affiliates are individuals or businesses that join the merchant's affiliate program to promote their products or services. They earn commissions or rewards for driving sales or other desired actions.

*Customer: The end consumer who purchases a product or service through an affiliate's promotional efforts.

2. Affiliate Program Setup: The merchant sets up an affiliate program, either in-house or through an affiliate network. The program includes details such as commission rates, payment terms, marketing materials, and tracking mechanisms.

3. Affiliate Promotion: Affiliates sign up for the merchant's affiliate program and receive unique tracking links or affiliate IDs. They use these links to promote the merchant's products or services through various marketing channels, such as websites, blogs, social media, email marketing, or paid advertising.

4. Tracking and Attribution: When a potential customer clicks on an affiliate's tracking link or uses their affiliate ID, a tracking cookie or code is stored on the user's device. This enables the merchant to track the customer's activity and attribute the sale or action to the respective affiliate.

5. Conversion and Sale: If the customer makes a purchase or completes a desired action (e.g., filling out a form, subscribing to a service) within a defined conversion window, the sale or action is attributed to the affiliate who referred the customer.

6. Commission and Rewards: Once the conversion is confirmed, the merchant calculates the commission or reward based on the agreed-upon terms and pays the affiliate accordingly. Commission structures can be based on a percentage of the sale value, a fixed amount per sale, or other criteria.

7. Performance Monitoring and Optimization: Merchants track the performance of their affiliate program, monitoring metrics such as sales, conversion rates, and affiliate-generated traffic. They may provide affiliates with reporting tools and performance metrics to help them optimize their marketing efforts.

8. Affiliate Program Management: Merchants actively manage their affiliate program, recruit new affiliates, provide support and resources, and ensure compliance with program terms. Affiliate networks may also provide assistance in managing the program and facilitating communication between affiliates and merchants.

Affiliate marketing has become a popular and effective

strategy for merchants to drive sales and for affiliates to monetize their online presence or marketing skills. It provides a mutually beneficial relationship where affiliates earn income, merchants gain exposure and sales, and customers discover relevant products or services through trusted recommendations.

Evolution and growth of the affiliate marketing industry

The affiliate marketing industry has experienced significant evolution and growth over the years, becoming a multi-billion dollar industry that continues to expand and innovate. Let's explore the key aspects of its evolution and growth.

Origins of Affiliate Marketing:

Affiliate marketing has its roots in traditional referral programs, where businesses rewarded individuals for referring customers. In the early days of the internet, this concept was applied to online platforms, and the first affiliate programs emerged. Amazon's Associates program, launched in 1996, is often credited as one of the pioneers of affiliate marketing.

Broadening Online Presence:

As the internet grew and e-commerce gained popularity, more businesses recognized the potential of affiliate marketing to drive sales and expand their online presence. This led to the proliferation of affiliate programs across various industries and verticals.

Technological Advancements:

Technological advancements played a crucial role in the growth of the affiliate marketing industry. The development of tracking technologies, such as cookies and unique affiliate links, enabled accurate tracking of referrals and ensured proper commission attribution. This boosted trust and transparency in the industry.

Affiliate Networks:

Affiliate networks emerged as intermediaries between merchants and affiliates, providing a platform for affiliate programs to connect with publishers. These networks streamlined the process by offering a centralized hub for tracking, reporting, and payment management. Popular affiliate networks include Commission Junction, ShareASale, and Rakuten Affiliate Network.

Diversification of Affiliate Models:

Initially, affiliate marketing primarily focused on cost-per-sale (CPS) models, where affiliates earned a commission for every sale generated. However, the industry diversified to include other models such as cost-per-action (CPA), where affiliates are rewarded for specific actions like filling out a form or signing up for a trial. This allowed for greater flexibility and expanded opportunities for affiliates.

Influencer Marketing:

The rise of social media platforms and the growth of influencer marketing have had a significant impact on the affiliate marketing industry. Influencers leverage their online presence and credibility to promote products and services, earning commissions through affiliate links. This has opened up a new avenue for brands to reach their target audience and drive sales.

Mobile and Cross-Device Tracking:

With the increasing use of mobile devices, affiliate marketing adapted to cater to this shift. Mobile tracking solutions emerged, allowing affiliates to track and monetize mobile traffic effectively. Additionally, cross-device tracking became essential, enabling affiliates to receive credit for referrals that spanned multiple devices, ensuring fair compensation.

Data Analytics and Optimization:

The availability of advanced analytics tools and data-driven insights has empowered both affiliates and merchants to optimize their strategies. Affiliates can track and analyze performance metrics, such as click-through rates and conversion rates, to refine their promotional efforts. Similarly, merchants can use data to identify high-performing affiliates and optimize their affiliate programs.

Integration of AI and Automation:

Artificial intelligence (AI) and automation have revolutionized the affiliate marketing industry. AI-powered algorithms can analyze vast amounts of data, predict trends, and make personalized recommendations, enhancing targeting and conversion rates. Automation tools help streamline repetitive tasks, such as link generation and reporting, freeing up time for affiliates to focus on strategy and content creation.

Global Expansion and Regulation:

Affiliate marketing has experienced significant growth on a global scale. Affiliates and merchants now operate in multiple countries, taking advantage of global markets. However, with growth comes increased regulatory scrutiny. Governments and regulatory bodies have implemented guidelines and regulations to ensure transparency, fair practices, and consumer protection within the industry.

The affiliate marketing industry has evolved from its early stages as a referral program to become a sophisticated and thriving industry. Technological advancements, influencer marketing, data analytics, and the integration of AI have propelled its growth. With continued innovation, the industry is poised

Benefits and advantages of affiliate marketing for businesses and individuals

Affiliate marketing offers several benefits and advantages for both businesses and individuals involved in the process. Here's a comprehensive explanation of these benefits:

Benefits for Businesses

1. Increased Reach: Affiliate marketing allows businesses

to expand their reach by leveraging the audience and networks of their affiliates. Affiliates promote the business's products or services to their own audience, reaching new potential customers that the business may not have been able to reach on its own.

2. Cost-Effective: Affiliate marketing is a performance-based marketing model, where businesses only pay affiliates when they successfully drive a desired action, such as a sale or lead. This makes it a cost-effective marketing strategy since businesses only pay for the actual results generated by the affiliates.

3. Enhanced Brand Visibility: By partnering with affiliates who have established online presence and credibility, businesses can significantly enhance their brand visibility. Affiliates promote the business's products or services through various channels, such as websites, blogs, social media, or email marketing, exposing the brand to a wider audience.

4. Targeted Marketing: Affiliates often have a niche or specific target audience that they cater to. By partnering with relevant affiliates, businesses can tap into these specific markets and target their ideal customer segments more effectively. This ensures that the marketing efforts are reaching the right audience, increasing the chances of conversions.

5. Improved SEO and Traffic: Affiliate marketing can contribute to search engine optimization (SEO) efforts and drive traffic to the business's website. Affiliate links and promotions on various platforms can generate backlinks, increasing the website's authority and improving its search engine rankings. Additionally, the referral traffic from affiliate websites can bring in new visitors who are already interested in the products or services being promoted.

Benefits for Individuals (Affiliates)

1. Passive Income: Affiliate marketing offers the opportunity for individuals to earn passive income. Once they set up their affiliate links or promotional materials, they can continue to earn commissions on sales or leads generated through their efforts, even when they're not actively promoting the products or services.

2. Flexibility and Freedom: Affiliate marketing provides individuals with the flexibility to work from anywhere and at their own pace. Affiliates have the freedom to choose which products or services they want to promote and how they want to promote them. This flexibility allows individuals to create their own schedules and pursue affiliate marketing alongside other commitments or businesses.

3. Low Startup Costs: Starting an affiliate marketing

business typically requires minimal investment. Affiliates don't need to create their own products or services, handle inventory, or deal with customer support. They can simply join affiliate programs and start promoting the products or services using the resources provided by the business.

4. Learning and Skill Development: Affiliate marketing offers individuals the opportunity to learn various marketing skills and strategies. Affiliates can gain experience in content creation, social media marketing, search engine optimization, email marketing, and more. These skills can be valuable for personal and professional growth, opening doors to other opportunities in the digital marketing industry.

5. Scalability and Unlimited Earning Potential: As affiliates gain experience and expand their reach, they can scale their affiliate marketing efforts. They can partner with multiple businesses, promote a wider range of products or services, and reach a larger audience. With effective strategies and a growing network, affiliates have the potential to earn unlimited commissions as their efforts and audience grows.

Affiliate marketing benefits businesses by increasing their reach, reducing marketing costs, enhancing brand visibility, and targeting specific markets. For individuals, it offers passive income opportunities, flexibility, low startup costs, skill development, and scalability. These advantages make affiliate marketing an appealing strategy for both businesses and individuals looking to grow their online presence and generate revenue.

CHAPTER TWO

Niche Selection and Market Research

Niche selection and market research are crucial steps in starting a successful business. They help you identify a target audience, understand their needs and preferences, and evaluate the potential profitability of a particular market segment. Let's delve into each of these areas in more detail.

Niche Selection

Choosing a niche involves finding a specific market segment that has unmet needs or underserved customers. Here are some steps to consider:

a. Identify your interests and expertise: Start by evaluating your own passions, knowledge, and skills. Consider industries or topics that you are genuinely interested in, as this will make the process more enjoyable and sustainable in the long run.

b. Evaluate market demand: Research the potential demand for products or services in your chosen niche. Look for market trends, growth potential, and any gaps or underserved areas that you could fill. Online tools, surveys, and social media platforms can provide insights into customer preferences and behavior.

c. Assess competition: Analyze the competition within your chosen niche. Identify the key players, their strengths and weaknesses, and the strategies they employ. Look for opportunities to differentiate yourself and offer something unique to customers.

d. Consider profitability: Evaluate the potential profitability of your niche by analyzing factors such as pricing, production costs, and profit margins. Ensure that the market is large enough and that customers are willing to pay for the value you provide.

Market Research

Once you've selected a niche, conducting thorough market research is crucial to gain a deeper understanding of your target market. Here are the key steps involved:

a. Define your target audience: Clearly identify your ideal customer profile. Consider demographics (age, gender, location), psychographics (interests, values, lifestyle), and any specific pain points or challenges your product or service can address.

b. Gather data: Use a combination of primary and secondary research methods to collect relevant data. Primary research involves collecting information directly from your target audience through surveys, interviews, or focus groups. Secondary research involves analyzing existing data from market reports, industry publications, and online sources.

c. Analyze customer needs: Understand the needs, desires, and motivations of your target audience. Identify their pain points, challenges, and goals to determine how your product or service can provide a solution or value proposition.

d. Evaluate market size and trends: Determine the size of your target market and its growth potential. Analyze industry trends, market forecasts, and any external factors that may impact your business, such as technological advancements, regulatory changes, or economic shifts.

e. Assess pricing and positioning: Determine appropriate pricing strategies based on your target audience's willingness to pay and your costs. Additionally, consider how you can position your offering relative to competitors to highlight its unique features or benefits.

f. Test and validate: Before launching your product or service, consider conducting market tests or running pilot programs to gather feedback from your target audience. This will help you refine your offering and ensure that it meets customer expectations.

Remember that niche selection and market research are ongoing processes. As your business evolves, continue to monitor the market, adapt to changing customer needs, and refine your strategies to maintain a competitive edge.

Importance of choosing a profitable niche

Choosing a profitable niche is of utmost importance for an affiliate marketer. It lays the foundation for your success and can significantly impact your ability to generate income. Here are several key reasons why selecting a profitable niche is crucial:

1. Higher Earning Potential: By targeting a profitable niche, you increase your chances of earning substantial commissions. Profitable niches typically have a higher demand for products or services, meaning there is a larger customer base to tap into. With more potential

customers, you have greater opportunities to drive sales and earn higher affiliate commissions.

2. Increased Conversion Rates: When you focus on a profitable niche, you can tailor your marketing efforts to a specific audience. This allows you to better understand their needs, preferences, and pain points. By catering your content and promotional strategies to their interests, you can improve your conversion rates. When your audience feels that you understand their needs and can provide valuable solutions, they are more likely to trust your recommendations and make a purchase through your affiliate links.

3. Competitive Advantage: Choosing a profitable niche with lower competition gives you a competitive edge. Highly saturated niches may be challenging to penetrate, as numerous marketers are vying for the same audience. On the other hand, by targeting a profitable niche with less competition, you can establish yourself as an authority and dominate the market. This enables you to build stronger relationships with your audience and stand out from the competition.

4. Long-Term Viability: A profitable niche is one that has sustainable demand over time. When selecting a niche, it's crucial to consider its long-term viability. Trends and fads may come and go, but choosing a niche with

enduring appeal ensures that your affiliate marketing efforts will remain relevant and profitable in the long run. Conduct thorough market research to assess the niche's potential for growth and longevity.

5. Monetization Opportunities: Profitable niches often offer diverse monetization opportunities. Beyond affiliate marketing, you may find opportunities for sponsored content, advertising, partnerships, or even creating and selling your own products or services. By selecting a niche with multiple revenue streams, you can maximize your earnings and create a sustainable business model.

6. Personal Interest and Expertise: While profitability is essential, it's also crucial to choose a niche that aligns with your interests and expertise. Building an affiliate marketing business requires dedication, effort, and consistent content creation. By selecting a niche you are passionate about, you will find it easier to stay motivated and produce high-quality content. Moreover, your genuine enthusiasm will resonate with your audience and enhance your credibility as an affiliate marketer.

Choosing a profitable niche as an affiliate marketer is vital for your success. It not only increases your earning potential but also allows you to target a specific audience, improve conversion rates, gain a competitive advantage, ensure long-term viability, and explore various monetization opportunities. By balancing profitability with personal interest and expertise, you can build a sustainable affiliate marketing business that generates substantial income and provides value to your audience.

Methods for identifying profitable niches

As an affiliate marketer, identifying profitable niches is crucial for the success of your business. Here are some methods and steps you can follow to identify profitable niches:

1. Market Research: Conduct thorough market research to identify trends, consumer demands, and emerging markets. Look for industries that are growing rapidly and have a substantial customer base. Use tools like Google Trends, industry reports, and keyword research tools to gather data and insights.

2. Passion and Knowledge: Consider your own interests, knowledge, and expertise. It's often easier to market products or services in niches that you are passionate

about or have experience in. Assess your skills, hobbies, and areas of expertise that can align with potential niches.

3. Target Audience Analysis: Identify your target audience and their pain points. Understand their needs, desires, and problems that need solving. Conduct surveys, interviews, and engage with your potential audience on social media platforms or forums to gather valuable insights.

4. Competition Analysis: Analyze the competition in potential niches. Look for niches with less competition or areas where you can differentiate yourself. Study successful affiliate marketers in your chosen niche to understand their strategies, products, and promotions. This analysis can help you identify gaps in the market that you can fulfill.

5. Affiliate Program Research: Look for affiliate programs or networks that offer products or services related to your chosen niche. Evaluate the commission rates, cookie duration, conversion rates, and support provided by different programs. Choose reputable affiliate programs that align with your niche and offer attractive earning potential.

6. Profitability Assessment: Assess the potential profitability of a niche by considering factors such as the

average order value, customer lifetime value, and potential recurring commissions. Evaluate if the niche has products or services with high-profit margins or if there are opportunities for upselling or cross-selling.

7. Keyword Research: Conduct keyword research to identify popular search terms related to your niche. Use tools like Google Keyword Planner, SEMrush, or Ahrefs to discover relevant keywords with high search volume and low competition. This research will help you understand the demand for products or services in your chosen niche.

8. Affiliate Network Insights: Leverage the insights provided by affiliate networks. Some networks provide data on top-performing niches, products, or offers. This information can give you a better understanding of niches that are currently profitable and in-demand.

9. Longevity and Sustainability: Consider the longevity and sustainability of the niche. Look for niches that have a long-term growth potential rather than short-lived trends. Sustainable niches will provide you with a consistent revenue stream over time.

10. Test and Evaluate: Once you have identified potential niches, test them on a smaller scale. Create a website or landing page, promote relevant products, and track the performance. Evaluate the conversion

rates, click-through rates, and profitability. Based on the results, optimize your strategies or pivot to a different niche if necessary.

Remember, identifying profitable niches requires a combination of research, analysis, and experimentation. Stay up-to-date with industry trends, consumer behavior, and continuously adapt your strategies to stay ahead of the competition.

Conducting market research to validate niche selection

Market research is a crucial step in validating your niche selection as an affiliate marketer. It helps you understand your target audience, their needs and preferences, and the potential demand for products or services in your chosen niche. Conducting comprehensive market research involves several key steps:

1. Identify Your Target Audience: Start by defining the specific group of people you want to target as an affiliate marketer. Consider factors such as age, gender, location, interests, and online behavior. Understanding your target audience will help you tailor your marketing

efforts and select relevant products or services.

2. Analyze Competitors: Research and analyze other affiliate marketers operating in your chosen niche. Identify their strategies, target audience, the products or services they promote, and their strengths and weaknesses. This analysis will help you identify gaps in the market and opportunities to differentiate yourself.

3. Evaluate Demand: Assess the demand for products or services in your niche. Look for search volume data using tools like Google Trends, keyword research tools, or social media listening tools. Determine if there is consistent interest in your niche over time and identify any seasonal or cyclical patterns.

4. Identify Affiliate Programs: Research and evaluate affiliate programs relevant to your niche. Look for reputable programs that offer competitive commissions, quality products or services, strong affiliate support, and reliable tracking and reporting systems. Joining established affiliate programs will increase your chances of success.

5. Engage with Your Audience: Interact with potential customers in your niche to gain insights into their needs and preferences. Join relevant online communities, forums, or social media groups and participate in discussions. Ask questions, provide valuable insights,

and listen to what your target audience is saying. This will help you understand their pain points and identify opportunities for affiliate marketing.

6. Assess Profitability: Consider the profitability of your chosen niche. Evaluate the average commission rates, potential sales volume, and the price points of products or services. Determine if the affiliate commissions will be sufficient to generate a desirable income based on your marketing efforts and the size of your target audience.

7. Validate Your Findings: Once you have gathered all the necessary information, validate your findings by conducting small-scale tests. Promote a few products or services in your niche and measure the response. Monitor metrics such as click-through rates, conversion rates, and affiliate earnings. Adjust your approach based on the results and feedback you receive.

8. Adapt and Evolve: Market research is an ongoing process. Continuously monitor market trends, consumer behavior, and competition in your niche. Stay updated with industry news and changes that may impact your affiliate marketing strategy. Adapt your approach as needed to stay relevant and meet the evolving needs of your target audience.

Remember, comprehensive market research is essential

for successful niche selection as an affiliate marketer. It helps you make informed decisions, understand your target audience, and identify opportunities for growth. By investing time and effort into thorough research, you increase your chances of building a profitable affiliate marketing business.

Tools and resources for niche research

As an affiliate marketer, conducting niche research is a crucial step in identifying profitable markets and selecting suitable products to promote. Here are some tools and resources that can assist you in conducting thorough niche research:

1. Google Trends: This tool allows you to explore the popularity of specific keywords over time, providing insights into seasonal trends and long-term interest. It can help you identify whether a niche is growing or declining in popularity.

2. Keyword Research Tools: Tools like Google Keyword Planner, SEMrush, and Ahrefs can provide data on search volume, competition, and related keywords. They can help you discover relevant keywords and assess the

level of competition in your chosen niche.

3. Niche-Specific Forums and Communities: Engaging in niche-specific forums and communities, such as Reddit, Quora, and specialized online forums, can provide valuable insights into the needs, preferences, and challenges of your target audience. It can also help you identify popular products and trends within your niche.

4. Competitor Analysis Tools: Tools like SEMrush, SimilarWeb, and SpyFu allow you to analyze your competitors' websites, traffic sources, keywords, and backlinks. This information can help you understand what strategies are working for successful affiliates in your niche.

5. Social Media Platforms: Platforms like Facebook, Twitter, Instagram, and LinkedIn can be useful for researching niche trends and understanding your target audience. Join relevant groups, follow influencers, and observe discussions to gain insights into popular products and emerging trends.

6. Affiliate Networks: Explore affiliate networks such as Amazon Associates, ClickBank, ShareASale, and CJ Affiliate to find products and programs related to your niche. These networks often provide data on commission rates, product popularity, and performance metrics to help you make informed decisions.

7. Consumer Research Tools: Tools like SurveyMonkey, Google Forms, and Typeform enable you to create surveys to gather feedback and insights from your target audience. This can help you understand their preferences, pain points, and buying behavior.

8. Google Analytics: Install Google Analytics on your website to track user behavior, traffic sources, and conversion rates. This data can help you identify the effectiveness of your marketing efforts and make data-driven decisions.

9. Trend Watching: Stay updated with industry news, blogs, and publications relevant to your niche. This will help you identify emerging trends and capitalize on them before they become main stream.

10. Product Review Sites: Browse through product review websites, such as Consumer Reports, CNET, or niche-specific review sites, to understand consumer preferences, pros and cons of products, and popular brands.

Remember, niche research requires a combination of quantitative data analysis and qualitative understanding of your target audience. Utilize these tools and resources to gather both types of information and make informed decisions about the profitability and viability of your chosen niche.

CHAPTER THREE

Building a Platform

Building a platform as an affiliate marketer involves creating a website or online presence that serves as a hub for promoting and selling products or services from other companies. As an affiliate marketer, your goal is to earn commissions by driving traffic and generating sales for the products or services you are promoting. Here are the steps involved in building such a platform:

1. Niche Selection: Choose a specific niche or industry that you are passionate about or have expertise in. This will help you focus your efforts and target a specific audience. Selecting a niche with high demand and profitability is also important.

2. Market Research: Conduct thorough market research to identify popular products or services within your chosen niche. Look for products that have a good reputation, high demand, and competitive commission rates. Consider using affiliate networks like Amazon

Associates, ShareASale, or CJ Affiliate to find suitable products to promote.

3. Domain Name and Hosting: Choose a domain name that reflects your niche and is easy to remember. Register the domain name with a reliable domain registrar and set up web hosting with a reputable hosting provider. Word Press is a popular content management system (CMS) that can be used for building your affiliate marketing platform.

4. Website Design and Development: Design a user-friendly and visually appealing website that aligns with your niche. Use a responsive design to ensure your website looks good on all devices. Install and customize a suitable Word Press theme, and add necessary functionalities using plugins. Include essential pages such as a homepage, about page, contact page, and product/service review pages.

5. Content Creation: Create high-quality content related to your niche that provides value to your audience. This can include blog posts, articles, product reviews, tutorials, videos, and more. Optimize your content for search engines by using relevant keywords and providing informative and engaging material.

6. Affiliate Program Selection: Join affiliate programs offered by companies whose products or services you

want to promote. Research the commission rates, cookie durations, and payment terms of different programs. Consider signing up for multiple programs to diversify your income streams.

7. Affiliate Link Integration: Generate unique affiliate links for the products or services you are promoting. Insert these links strategically within your content, such as in product reviews or relevant articles. When visitors click on these links and make a purchase, you earn a commission.

8. SEO Optimization: Optimize your website for search engines to improve its visibility and organic traffic. Conduct keyword research to identify relevant keywords for your content. Incorporate these keywords naturally into your content, including titles, headings, meta descriptions, and alt tags. Build quality backlinks through guest posting, social media promotion, and outreach to improve your website's authority.

9. Promotion and Marketing: Implement various marketing strategies to drive traffic to your platform. This can include social media marketing, email marketing, paid advertising, influencer collaborations, content promotion, and search engine marketing. Tailor your marketing efforts to reach your target audience effectively.

10. Analytics and Optimization: Track the performance of your affiliate marketing platform using tools like Google Analytics. Monitor your website traffic, click-through rates, conversion rates, and earnings. Analyze the data to identify successful strategies and areas for improvement. Optimize your content and marketing efforts based on the insights gained.

11. Continuous Learning and Adaptation: Stay updated with industry trends, changes in affiliate programs, and emerging marketing techniques. Attend conferences, webinars, and join relevant communities to expand your knowledge. Adapt your strategies accordingly to stay competitive and maximize your earning potential.

Remember, building a successful affiliate marketing platform takes time, effort, and persistence. It requires consistently providing value to your audience, promoting quality products or services, and refining your strategies based on data and feedback. With dedication and the right approach, you can create a thriving affiliate marketing business.

Setting up a professional and user-friendly platform

Setting up a professional and user-friendly platform as an affiliate marketer is essential for attracting and retaining your audience. Here's a step-by-step guide on how to do it:

1. Choose a Niche: Select a specific niche or industry that aligns with your interests, expertise, and market demand. Focusing on a niche helps you target a specific audience and establish yourself as an authority in that area.

2. Register a Domain: Choose a domain name that is relevant to your niche and represents your brand. Opt for a domain extension like .com, .org, or .net, as they are widely recognized and trusted. You can register a domain through domain registrars like GoDaddy or Namecheap.

3. Web Hosting: Find a reliable web hosting provider to store your website's files and make it accessible on the internet. Look for a hosting package that offers good performance, uptime, security, and scalability. Popular hosting providers include Bluehost, SiteGround, and HostGator.

4. Content Management System (CMS): Install a CMS to build and manage your website easily. Word Press is a popular choice as it offers a user-friendly interface, a wide range of themes and plugins, and great flexibility. Most hosting providers have one-click Word Press installations, making it easy to set up.

5. Design and Customization: Choose a professional and visually appealing theme for your website. Word Press offers numerous free and premium themes that you can customize to match your brand's colors, logo, and overall aesthetic. Ensure your website design is responsive, meaning it adapts to different screen sizes for optimal user experience.

6. Content Creation: Create high-quality, engaging, and informative content related to your niche. This could include blog posts, articles, product reviews, tutorials, videos, and more. Optimize your content for search engines by incorporating relevant keywords, meta tags, and headings. Regularly update your website with fresh content to keep visitors coming back.

7. Affiliate Network Selection: Join reputable affiliate networks that offer products or services relevant to your niche. Some popular affiliate networks include Amazon Associates, ShareASale, CJ Affiliate, and ClickBank. These platforms provide access to a wide range of affiliate

programs, track your affiliate links, and provide performance analytics.

8. Affiliate Link Placement: Strategically place your affiliate links within your content. Ensure they are contextually relevant and add value to the user experience. Avoid excessive use of affiliate links, as it can appear spammy and turn off your audience. Disclose your affiliate relationships transparently to maintain trust with your visitors.

9. Optimize for Conversion: Implement conversion optimization techniques to maximize your affiliate earnings. Use compelling calls-to-action (CTAs), create comparison tables, include product images, and highlight the benefits of the products or services you promote. Split testing different approaches can help you identify what works best for your audience.

10. Build an Email List: Offer valuable content upgrades or incentives to encourage visitors to subscribe to your email list. This allows you to build a loyal audience and promote affiliate products or special offers directly to their inbox. Utilize email marketing tools like Mailchimp or ConvertKit to manage your email campaigns effectively.

11. Social Media Presence: Establish a strong presence on social media platforms relevant to your niche. Share

your content, engage with your audience, and promote affiliate products through social media posts. Use social media management tools like Hootsuite or Buffer to schedule and automate your posts.

12. Analytics and Tracking: Set up website analytics using tools like Google Analytics. Monitor your website's performance, track user behavior, and analyze conversion rates. This data helps you make data-driven decisions, optimize your content, and identify areas for improvement.

13. Website Security: Implement security measures to protect your website and your users' data. Use SSL certificates to enable HTTPS encryption

Essential elements of an effective affiliate marketing platform

An effective affiliate marketing platform is a crucial tool for businesses to expand their reach, increase sales, and build partnerships with affiliate marketers. It provides a streamlined system for managing and tracking affiliate activities. Here are the essential elements of an effective affiliate marketing platform with comprehensive explanations:

1. User-Friendly Interface: The platform should have an intuitive and user-friendly interface that allows both merchants and affiliates to easily navigate through the system. Clear navigation menus, well-organized dashboards, and easy-to-use features contribute to a positive user experience.

2. Affiliate Management System: The platform should include a robust affiliate management system that enables businesses to manage their affiliate programs efficiently. This system allows merchants to onboard affiliates, track their performance, provide them with marketing assets, and communicate with them effectively.

3. Tracking and Analytics: Accurate tracking and analytics are vital for affiliate marketing success. The platform should provide reliable tracking mechanisms to monitor affiliate performance, such as tracking links, cookies, or unique promo codes. It should also offer comprehensive analytics tools to measure key performance indicators (KPIs), such as conversions, click-through rates, and revenue generated by each affiliate.

4. Commission and Payment Management: An effective affiliate marketing platform should have a flexible

commission and payment management system. It should allow merchants to set commission rates, define commission structures (e.g., flat rates or percentage-based), and automate commission calculations. The platform should also support multiple payment methods and provide transparent reporting on commissions earned and paid out to affiliates.

5. Marketing Tools and Resources: To empower affiliates and enhance their promotional efforts, the platform should offer a range of marketing tools and resources. This may include access to a library of promotional materials such as banners, text links, email templates, and product catalogs. Advanced platforms may also provide additional features like deep linking capabilities or content creation tools.

6. Communication and Support: Effective communication channels and support are crucial for successful affiliate partnerships. The platform should facilitate communication between merchants and affiliates, allowing them to exchange messages, share updates, and provide support when needed. This can be in the form of an integrated messaging system, email notifications, or even a dedicated support team.

7. Fraud Prevention and Security: An affiliate marketing platform should prioritize fraud prevention and security

measures to protect both merchants and affiliates. This may include fraud detection algorithms, affiliate verification processes, secure payment gateways, and data encryption to safeguard sensitive information.

8. Integration and Scalability: The platform should be easily integrable with other marketing tools, e-commerce platforms, and analytics solutions. It should also be scalable to accommodate the growing needs of businesses and support a large number of affiliates. API integrations and customization options are essential for seamless integration with existing systems.

9. Real-Time Reporting and Insights: Real-time reporting and insights are crucial for monitoring campaign performance and making data-driven decisions. The platform should provide merchants and affiliates with comprehensive reports and analytics dashboards, allowing them to track performance, identify trends, and optimize their strategies in real-time.

10. Affiliate Recruitment and Networking: To foster affiliate partnerships, the platform should offer features for affiliate recruitment and networking. This can include directories or marketplaces where affiliates can discover and apply to join relevant programs. Additionally, the platform can provide networking opportunities such as forums or events where affiliates

can connect with merchants and share insights.

By incorporating these essential elements into an affiliate marketing platform, businesses can effectively manage their affiliate programs, foster fruitful partnerships, and drive significant results in terms of traffic, conversions, and revenue.

CHAPTER FOUR

Content Creation and SEO

Content creation and SEO (Search Engine Optimization) are two closely related concepts that play crucial roles in online marketing and digital presence. Let's delve into each of these concepts and explore how they work together to drive organic traffic and enhance a website's visibility on search engines.

Content Creation

Content creation refers to the process of generating valuable and engaging material for various platforms such as websites, blogs, social media, videos, and more. The aim of content creation is to provide relevant and valuable information to the target audience, establish credibility, and ultimately drive desired actions such as conversions or brand loyalty.

Effective content creation involves several key

elements

1. Understanding the Target Audience: It's essential to have a clear understanding of the target audience, their needs, preferences, and pain points. This knowledge helps in crafting content that resonates with the intended audience and provides them with relevant solutions or information.

2. Keyword Research: Keyword research involves identifying the specific words or phrases that users search for on search engines when looking for information related to your industry or niche. Thorough keyword research helps in understanding the language and terms used by your target audience, allowing you to optimize your content accordingly.

3. Valuable and Engaging Content: Creating high-quality content that adds value to the audience is crucial. This can be in the form of informative articles, instructional videos, entertaining podcasts, or visually appealing info-graphics. Engaging content helps in capturing and retaining the attention of users, encouraging them to spend more time on your website and increasing the likelihood of conversions.

4. Consistency: Consistently producing fresh and relevant content is key to maintaining an engaged audience. Regularly updated content signals to search

engines that your website is active and provides value, which can positively impact your search engine rankings.

Search Engine Optimization (SEO)

SEO is the practice of optimizing your website and its content to improve its visibility and ranking on search engine results pages (SERPs). The ultimate goal of SEO is to drive organic (non-paid) traffic to your website by appearing higher in search engine rankings.

Here are some important elements of SEO:

1. On-Page Optimization: On-page optimization involves optimizing various aspects of your website and its individual pages to make them search engine-friendly. This includes optimizing Meta tags (title tags, Meta descriptions), headings, URL structure, internal linking, and ensuring keyword relevance throughout the content.

2. Off-Page Optimization: Off-page optimization focuses on improving your website's authority and reputation through external factors. This primarily involves acquiring backlinks from other reputable websites, as search engines consider backlinks as indicators of a website's credibility and relevance.

3. Technical SEO: Technical SEO involves optimizing the technical aspects of your website to improve its crawl

ability and index ability by search engines. This includes optimizing site speed, mobile responsiveness, XML sitemaps, robots.txt file, and ensuring proper website structure.

4. User Experience: Providing a positive user experience is crucial for SEO. Factors such as website load speed, mobile-friendliness, easy navigation, and engaging content all contribute to a better user experience. Search engines prioritize websites that offer a smooth and valuable experience to their users.

5. Analytics and Monitoring: Monitoring and analyzing your website's performance using tools like Google Analytics can provide valuable insights into user behavior, keyword performance, and overall website health. This data allows you to identify areas for improvement and make data-driven decisions to enhance your SEO efforts.

Integration of Content Creation and SEO

Content creation and SEO are tightly interconnected. While content creation focuses on providing valuable information to the target audience, SEO ensures that this content is discoverable by search engines and ranks well in relevant search queries.

To integrate content creation and SEO effectively,

consider the following:

Keyword Optimization: Conduct thorough keyword research to identify the relevant keywords to target within your content.

Importance of high-quality content in affiliate marketing

High-quality content plays a crucial role in the success of affiliate marketing. It serves as the foundation for building trust, attracting and engaging audiences, and ultimately driving conversions. Here are some comprehensive explanations highlighting the importance of high-quality content in affiliate marketing:

1. Establishing Trust: High-quality content helps establish trust with your audience. By providing valuable and reliable information, you position yourself as an authority in your niche. When visitors perceive you as knowledgeable and trustworthy, they are more likely to follow your recommendations and click on your affiliate links.

2. Building Credibility: Creating well-researched and informative content demonstrates your expertise and

credibility in the field. When you consistently deliver high-quality content, readers perceive you as a reliable source of information. This credibility enhances the likelihood of them considering your recommendations and making purchases through your affiliate links.

3. Increasing Traffic: Search engines favor high-quality content. By producing valuable and relevant content, you increase your chances of ranking higher in search engine results. This, in turn, drives organic traffic to your website or blog, exposing more people to your affiliate links and increasing the likelihood of conversions.

4. Engaging and Retaining Audiences: Compelling content captivates your audience and keeps them engaged. By addressing their needs, answering their questions, and providing helpful insights, you can create a loyal following. Engaged readers are more likely to spend time on your site, explore your recommendations, and convert into customers.

5. Enhancing Conversions: High-quality content has the power to persuade and influence purchasing decisions. When your content educates, informs, and entertains, it builds a connection with your audience. By strategically integrating relevant affiliate links within your content, you can recommend products or services that genuinely address your readers' needs, increasing the likelihood of

conversions.

6. Differentiating Yourself: In the saturated world of affiliate marketing, high-quality content can set you apart from competitors. By producing unique, valuable, and insightful content, you create a distinct voice and brand identity. This uniqueness helps you stand out, attract a loyal audience, and develop a competitive edge.

7. Generating Repeat Business: When you consistently produce high-quality content, you encourage repeat visits from your audience. Returning visitors are more likely to engage with your affiliate links, leading to recurring commissions. Additionally, satisfied customers may share your content with others, expanding your reach and potential customer base.

8. Adhering to Ethical Standards: Affiliate marketing requires transparency and honesty. By creating high-quality content, you can provide accurate and unbiased information about the products or services you promote. This ethical approach builds trust with your audience, leading to long-term relationships and sustainable success.

Overall, high-quality content forms the backbone of successful affiliate marketing. It helps you establish trust, build credibility, increase traffic, engage and retain audiences, enhance conversions, differentiate yourself from competitors, generate repeat business, and adhere to ethical standards. By investing time and effort into creating valuable content, you can maximize the potential of your affiliate marketing endeavors.

Strategies for creating engaging and informative content

As an affiliate marketer, creating engaging and informative content is crucial for attracting and retaining your audience. Here are some strategies to help you achieve that:

1. Understand your audience: To create engaging content, you need to understand your target audience's needs, preferences, and pain points. Conduct thorough market research, analyze customer data, and engage with your audience through surveys or social media to gather insights. This understanding will enable you to create content that resonates with your audience.

2. Choose relevant and valuable products: Select products or services that are relevant to your audience's

interests and provide value to them. Prioritize quality over quantity, and focus on promoting products that you genuinely believe in and can vouch for. Your audience will appreciate your authenticity and trust your recommendations.

3. Write compelling headlines: A catchy and compelling headline is crucial for grabbing your audience's attention. Use strong, action-oriented language, and emphasize the benefits or solutions your content offers. Experiment with different headline formats, such as lists, how-tos, or questions, to pique curiosity and entice readers to click.

4. Create high-quality content: Your content should be well-written, well-structured, and provide valuable information to your audience. Use clear and concise language, break up text with subheadings and bullet points, and include visuals like images, infographics, or videos to enhance comprehension and engagement. Aim for a conversational tone to make your content more relatable.

5. Incorporate storytelling: Storytelling is a powerful tool for engaging your audience. Use personal anecdotes, case studies, or customer testimonials to illustrate the benefits or experiences related to the products you're promoting. Stories create an emotional connection with

readers and make your content more memorable.

6. Include actionable tips and advice: Provide practical advice and actionable tips that your audience can implement immediately. Break down complex concepts into easily digestible steps, and offer guidance on how to achieve specific goals or solve problems. This approach positions you as an authority and builds trust with your audience.

7. Use visuals and multimedia: Incorporate relevant visuals, such as images, charts, or infographics, to complement your written content. Visual elements make your content more engaging and help convey information more effectively. Additionally, consider using multimedia formats like videos or podcasts to diversify your content and cater to different learning preferences.

8. Optimize for SEO: Implement search engine optimization (SEO) techniques to improve the visibility of your content in search engine results. Conduct keyword research to identify relevant terms and phrases, and strategically incorporate them into your content, including headings, meta tags, and image alt text. This helps attract organic traffic and increases the chances of your content being discovered by your target audience.

9. Encourage interaction and feedback: Engage with your audience by encouraging comments, questions, and discussions. Respond promptly and thoughtfully to comments, and foster a sense of community around your content. This interaction not only helps build relationships but also provides valuable insights into your audience's needs and interests.

10. Continuously analyze and improve: Regularly monitor the performance of your content using analytics tools. Track metrics like page views, time on page, click-through rates, and conversion rates to understand what content resonates most with your audience. Use this data to refine your content strategy and make informed decisions on future topics and formats.

By implementing these strategies, you can create engaging and informative content that not only attracts and retains your audience but also drives conversions as an affiliate marketer. Remember to stay consistent, adapt to your audience's evolving needs, and always prioritize delivering value.

Search engine optimization (SEO) techniques to improve visibility and organic traffic

Search Engine Optimization (SEO) is the process of optimizing a website to improve its visibility and organic (non-paid) traffic from search engines. By implementing effective SEO techniques, you can enhance your website's chances of appearing in relevant search results and attracting more visitors. Here are some key SEO techniques that can help improve visibility and organic traffic:

1. Keyword Research: Keyword research is the foundation of SEO. It involves identifying the search terms and phrases that people use when looking for information related to your website's content. By targeting relevant keywords in your content, Meta tags, and URLs, you can increase your chances of ranking higher in search results.

2. On-Page Optimization: On-page optimization refers to optimizing individual web pages to make them more searches engine-friendly. This includes optimizing the page titles, headings, Meta tags, URLs, and content with relevant keywords. It's important to ensure that the

content is high-quality, informative, and meets the needs of your target audience.

3. Technical SEO: Technical SEO focuses on optimizing the technical aspects of your website to improve its visibility to search engines. This includes improving website speed and performance, ensuring mobile-friendliness and responsive design, optimizing site structure and navigation, and implementing proper URL structures. Technical SEO helps search engines crawl and index your website more effectively.

4. Link Building: Link building is the process of acquiring high-quality backlinks from other websites to your own. Search engines consider backlinks as a vote of confidence for your website's credibility and relevance. Building backlinks from reputable and relevant websites can improve your website's authority and visibility in search results. You can acquire backlinks through content creation, guest blogging, influencer outreach, and other link-building strategies.

5. Content Creation: Creating high-quality, unique, and relevant content is crucial for SEO. Search engines value fresh and engaging content that provides value to users. By regularly publishing informative articles, blog posts, videos, and other forms of content, you can attract more organic traffic and increase the likelihood of your

website being linked to and shared by others.

6. User Experience (UX): User experience plays a vital role in SEO. Search engines consider factors such as page load speed, mobile-friendliness, easy navigation, and overall user satisfaction when ranking websites. Optimizing your website for a seamless and enjoyable user experience can lead to higher engagement, longer visit durations, and lower bounce rates, all of which positively impact your SEO efforts.

7. Social Media Promotion: While social media signals may not directly impact search engine rankings, social media platforms can be powerful channels for promoting your content and reaching a wider audience. By sharing your content on social media platforms, engaging with your followers, and encouraging social sharing, you can increase brand visibility, attract more traffic, and potentially earn more backlinks.

8. Analytics and Monitoring: It's essential to monitor and analyze your website's performance using tools like Google Analytics. By tracking metrics such as organic traffic, keyword rankings, click-through rates, and bounce rates, you can identify areas for improvement and measure the effectiveness of your SEO strategies. Regular analysis allows you to make data-driven decisions to refine and optimize your SEO efforts.

Remember that SEO is a long-term strategy that requires ongoing effort and adaptation. It's important to stay up-to-date with the latest SEO trends and algorithm updates, as search engines continuously evolve their ranking criteria. By implementing these techniques and consistently providing value to your target audience, you can improve your website's visibility and organic traffic over time.

Utilizing keywords and optimizing on-page elements

When it comes to optimizing on-page elements and utilizing keywords for search engine optimization (SEO), there are several key factors to consider. Here are some best practices to follow:

1. Page Title: Include your primary keyword or phrase in the title tag of your web page. Keep the title concise, compelling, and relevant to the content. Ideally, keep it under 60 characters to ensure it displays properly in search engine results.

2. Meta Description: Write a concise and compelling meta description that accurately summarizes the content of the page. Although meta descriptions don't

directly impact rankings, they can influence click-through rates from search engine results pages (SERPs).

3. Heading Tags: Utilize heading tags (H1, H2, H3, etc.) to structure your content and make it easier for both users and search engines to understand. Incorporate relevant keywords into your headings, but ensure they flow naturally and don't appear forced.

4. URL Structure: Create SEO-friendly URLs that are descriptive and include keywords related to the page's content. Avoid long and convoluted URLs, and use hyphens to separate words.

5. Keyword Placement: Incorporate your target keywords throughout the content naturally. Include them in the first paragraph, headings, subheadings, and throughout the body of the text. However, avoid overstuffing keywords, as it can lead to penalties.

6. Image Optimization: Optimize images by using descriptive filenames and alt tags that include relevant keywords. Compress images to improve page load speed, as faster-loading pages are preferred by search engines.

7. Internal Linking: Include relevant internal links within your content to provide additional context and help search engines understand the structure and hierarchy

of your website. Anchor text of internal links should be descriptive and relevant.

8. Mobile-Friendly Design: Ensure your website is mobile-friendly and responsive, as mobile usability is a crucial ranking factor. Test your website's mobile compatibility and make necessary adjustments for a seamless mobile experience.

9. User Experience: Focus on creating high-quality, valuable content that engages and satisfies your users' intent. Search engines prioritize websites that deliver a positive user experience, so optimize your website for easy navigation, fast load times, and intuitive design.

Remember that SEO is an ongoing process, and it's essential to monitor your website's performance, make adjustments based on analytics data, and stay up to date with search engine algorithm changes.

CHAPTER FIVE

Finding and Joining Affiliate Programs

Affiliate programs are a popular way for individuals and businesses to earn money by promoting products or services offered by other companies. If you're interested in finding and joining affiliate programs, here's a comprehensive explanation of the process:

Understand Affiliate Marketing

Before diving into affiliate programs, it's essential to understand the basics of affiliate marketing. Affiliate marketing is a performance-based marketing strategy where affiliates earn a commission for each sale or action generated through their promotional efforts. As an affiliate, you'll be given unique tracking links or codes to track your referrals and earnings.

Identify Your Niche or Interest

To be successful in affiliate marketing, it's crucial to

focus on a niche or industry that aligns with your interests or expertise. By selecting a niche, you can target a specific audience and provide valuable content that resonates with them.

Research Affiliate Networks

Affiliate networks act as intermediaries between affiliates and companies offering affiliate programs. They provide a platform where you can find a wide range of affiliate programs from different companies. Some popular affiliate networks include:

*Amazon Associates: Offers a wide range of products from Amazon.com.

*ShareASale: Provides a diverse selection of programs across various industries.

*CJ Affiliate (formerly Commission Junction): Offers a large network of advertisers.

*ClickBank: Focuses on digital products such as e-books and online courses.

Research and explore these networks to find affiliate programs that suit your niche and interests.

Explore Direct Affiliate Programs

In addition to affiliate networks, many companies run

their own affiliate programs. If you have specific brands or products in mind that you'd like to promote, visit their websites and look for an "Affiliate Program" or "Partnership" link in the footer or header sections. This approach allows you to work directly with the company, often resulting in higher commission rates and personalized support.

Evaluate Program Details

Once you've found potential affiliate programs, carefully review their terms and conditions. Look for information about commission rates, payment methods, cookie duration (the time during which you'll earn a commission on a referral), and any specific program requirements. Consider factors like the reputation of the company, product quality, and affiliate support.

Sign Up and Get Approved

To join an affiliate program, you'll need to complete an application or sign-up process. This usually involves providing information about your website or promotional methods, traffic statistics, and how you plan to promote the products. Some programs may have certain eligibility criteria, such as minimum traffic requirements or content guidelines. Be honest and transparent in your application to increase your chances of approval.

Generate Affiliate Links and Start Promoting

Upon approval, you'll gain access to your affiliate dashboard, where you can generate unique tracking links or codes. These links are used to track the traffic and sales you generate. Integrate these links into your website, blog posts, social media profiles, email newsletters, or any other promotional channels you use. Remember to disclose your affiliate relationships to comply with legal regulations and maintain transparency with your audience.

Create Valuable Content

To effectively promote affiliate products, focus on creating high-quality content that provides value to your audience. This could include product reviews, tutorials, comparison articles, or informative guides related to your niche. By building trust and offering helpful information, you're more likely to drive conversions and earn commissions.

Monitor Performance and Optimize

Regularly monitor your affiliate performance through the reports and analytics provided by the affiliate network or program. Track metrics such as clicks, conversions, and earnings. Identify the most successful strategies and optimize your promotional efforts accordingly. Experiment with different types of content, marketing channels, and product selections to find what works best for you.

Researching and selecting reputable affiliate programs

When researching and selecting reputable affiliate programs, it's essential to consider several factors to ensure you choose a reliable and trustworthy program. Here's a step-by-step guide to help you in your research and selection process:

1. Define your niche or target audience: Determine the specific area or industry you want to focus on. This will help you narrow down your search for affiliate programs that align with your interests and expertise.

2. Research affiliate networks: Start by exploring reputable affiliate networks that act as intermediaries between affiliates and merchants. Some popular affiliate networks include Amazon Associates, Commission Junction, ShareASale, and ClickBank. These networks provide access to a wide range of affiliate programs

across various industries.

3. Consider the program's reputation: Look for affiliate programs with a solid reputation in the industry. Research the program's background, how long they have been operating, and their track record of payments and customer support. Reading reviews and testimonials from other affiliates can provide valuable insights.

4. Evaluate commission structure and payout terms: Examine the commission rates offered by the affiliate programs you're considering. Compare them to industry standards to ensure they are competitive. Additionally, review the payout terms, such as the minimum payment threshold and payment methods, to ensure they align with your preferences.

5. Assess the product or service quality: It's crucial to promote products or services that are reputable and of high quality. Look for affiliate programs that offer products or services that align with your audience's needs and have a positive reputation in the market. Consider factors such as customer reviews, product ratings, and the merchant's brand credibility.

6. Check affiliate support and resources: A good affiliate program should provide adequate support and resources to help you succeed. Look for programs that offer marketing materials, tracking tools, dedicated

affiliate managers, and educational resources such as tutorials or webinars. These resources can assist you in optimizing your marketing efforts and maximizing your earnings.

7. Review affiliate program policies: Carefully read and understand the program's terms and conditions, as well as their policies on issues such as cookie duration, attribution rules, and any restrictions on promotional methods. Ensure the program's policies align with your marketing strategies and goals.

8. Look for transparent reporting and tracking: A reputable affiliate program should provide accurate and transparent reporting and tracking of your referrals and commissions. Make sure the program offers robust tracking technology that allows you to monitor your performance effectively.

9. Consider program longevity and stability: While newer affiliate programs can be promising, it's generally safer to choose programs with a proven track record of stability and longevity. This reduces the risk of the program shutting down abruptly, leaving you without any earnings.

10. Seek recommendations and feedback: Reach out to other affiliates or industry experts for recommendations and feedback on the affiliate programs you are

considering. Online communities, forums, and social media groups dedicated to affiliate marketing can be valuable sources of insights and recommendations.

Remember that affiliate marketing success depends on various factors, including the quality of your content, your marketing strategies, and your audience engagement. Choosing a reputable affiliate program is just the first step toward building a successful affiliate marketing business.

Evaluating commission structures and payment methods

As an affiliate marketer, evaluating commission structures and payment methods is crucial for optimizing your earnings and ensuring a fair and reliable income stream. Let's break down these two aspects and provide a comprehensive explanation for each.

1. Commission Structures:

Commission structures determine how you earn money as an affiliate marketer. Here are some common types of commission structures:

a. Percentage-based Commission: This structure pays you a percentage of the total sale amount generated through your affiliate link. For example, if the commission rate is 10% and a customer purchases a $100 product through your link, you would earn $10.

b. Fixed Commission: With this structure, you earn a fixed amount for each referral or sale, regardless of the purchase value. For instance, you may receive $20 for every customer who signs up for a particular service through your link.

c. Tiered Commission: In a tiered commission structure, your commission rate increases as you reach higher sales or referral thresholds. This encourages you to drive more sales and rewards your performance with higher earnings.

d. Recurring Commission: Some affiliate programs offer recurring commissions, typically in subscription-based services. You earn a commission not only for the initial sale but also for each subsequent payment made by the referred customer.

e. Performance-based Commission: In this structure, your commission depends on predefined performance metrics, such as the number of clicks, leads, or conversions. The more successful you are in meeting these metrics, the higher your commission.

When evaluating commission structures, consider the following factors:

* Commission rates: Determine the percentage or fixed amount you will earn per sale or referral. Higher commission rates may be more appealing, but also consider the product or service's price point and conversion rate.

* Product or service quality: Ensure the products or services you promote align with your audience's interests and have a good reputation. High-quality offerings can lead to higher conversion rates and customer satisfaction.

* Cookie duration: Cookies track the user's referral source, allowing you to earn commissions even if the purchase happens later. Longer cookie durations increase the likelihood of earning commissions from delayed conversions.

* Attribution models: Understand how the affiliate program attributes sales to affiliates. Some programs use last-click attribution, crediting the commission to the last affiliate link clicked before the purchase. Others may use first-click or multi-touch attribution models.

2. Payment Methods:

Payment methods determine how you receive your commissions. Here are common payment methods used by affiliate programs:

a. PayPal: PayPal is a widely used online payment platform that offers quick and secure transactions. Many affiliate programs support PayPal as a payment method.

b. Direct Deposit: This method allows your commissions to be deposited directly into your bank account. It offers convenience and eliminates the need for additional intermediaries.

c. Wire Transfer: Wire transfers enable direct transfers of funds from the affiliate program's account to your bank account. They are useful for international affiliate marketers but may involve higher fees.

d. Check: Some programs still offer commission payments via physical checks, which are mailed to your registered address. Checks can be slower and may involve additional fees for international recipients.

When evaluating payment methods, consider the following factors:

* Convenience and accessibility: Choose payment methods that are easy to use and accessible in your

country or region. Ensure the payment method aligns with your preferences and financial needs.

* Payment threshold: Some programs have a minimum earnings threshold that must be reached before you can request a payout. Ensure the threshold is reasonable and achievable based on your marketing efforts.

* Payment frequency: Understand how often payments are made. Some programs offer weekly, bi-monthly, or monthly payments, while others may have longer payout cycles.

* Fees and charges: Consider any associated fees or charges with the payment method. These can include transaction fees, currency conversion fees, or withdrawal fees. Be aware of the impact these

Strategies for getting approved by affiliate networks and programs

Getting approved by affiliate networks and programs requires careful planning and execution. Here are some strategies to increase your chances of approval:

Affiliate Marketing Blueprint

1. Choose the Right Networks: Research and identify reputable affiliate networks that align with your niche or industry. Look for networks that have a solid reputation, good track record, and a wide range of advertisers.

2. Build a Professional Website: Create a well-designed website that reflects your professionalism and expertise. Make sure your website is visually appealing, easy to navigate, and mobile-friendly. It should also have clear and valuable content related to the products or services you intend to promote.

3. Produce Quality Content: Content is king in affiliate marketing. Create high-quality, engaging content that provides value to your target audience. This can include blog posts, videos, reviews, tutorials, or any other form of content that educates and informs users about the products or services you promote.

4. Focus on Traffic and Engagement: Affiliate networks want to see that you have a steady flow of traffic and engaged users. Work on driving targeted traffic to your website through various channels such as search engine optimization (SEO), social media marketing, email marketing, or paid advertising. Aim to build an engaged audience by encouraging comments, shares, and interactions on your content.

5. Demonstrate Your Expertise: Position yourself as an

authority in your niche by consistently creating valuable and informative content. Show that you have in-depth knowledge about the products or services you intend to promote. This will help establish trust with both the affiliate networks and your audience.

6. Build an Email List: One effective way to demonstrate your marketing potential is by building an email list. Capture visitor emails using lead magnets or opt-in forms on your website. Growing your email list shows that you have a dedicated audience and a means to reach them directly.

7. Be Transparent and Compliant: Affiliate networks value transparency and compliance. Make sure you clearly disclose any affiliate relationships to your audience. Follow ethical practices and adhere to the guidelines set by both the affiliate networks and the Federal Trade Commission (FTC).

8. Provide Performance Metrics: If you have an existing affiliate marketing track record, share your performance metrics with the affiliate networks. This includes conversion rates, average order value, click-through rates, or any other relevant data that demonstrates your ability to generate results.

9. Personalize Your Application: When applying to affiliate networks, personalize your application and

explain why you are interested in their network specifically. Show that you've done your research and understand how their network can benefit both you and the advertisers.

10. Be Patient and Persistent: Getting approved by affiliate networks can sometimes take time. If you get rejected initially, don't get discouraged. Review the feedback provided, make improvements if necessary, and reapply. Persistence pays off in the long run.

Remember, each affiliate network and program may have its own specific requirements and criteria. It's crucial to review their guidelines and tailor your approach accordingly. Building a strong online presence, providing value to your audience and showcasing your expertise are key factors that can significantly increase your chances of getting approved by affiliate networks and programs.

Tips for negotiating higher commissions and exclusive deals

Negotiating higher commissions and exclusive deals as

an affiliate marketer requires a strategic approach. Here are some tips to help you in your negotiations:

1. Understand your value: Before entering into negotiations, analyze the value you bring to the table. Consider factors such as your audience size, engagement rates, conversion rates, and the quality of your content. The stronger your value proposition, the more leverage you'll have in negotiations.

2. Research and compare: Conduct thorough research on the industry and the affiliate programs you're interested in. Look for programs that offer competitive commissions and exclusive deals. Compare different programs to understand the range of possibilities and identify benchmarks for your negotiations.

3. Showcase your track record: Highlight your past successes as an affiliate marketer. Provide data and evidence of your performance, such as conversion rates, click-through rates, and revenue generated for previous campaigns. This information can demonstrate your ability to drive results and justify higher commissions or exclusive offers.

4. Build relationships: Develop strong relationships with affiliate managers and program representatives. Regularly communicate with them, provide feedback, and show your commitment to their program. Building

rapport and trust can enhance your negotiating position and increase your chances of securing better deals.

5. Propose win-win solutions: When negotiating, focus on creating win-win situations. Offer creative suggestions that benefit both parties involved. For example, you can propose higher commissions in exchange for exclusivity or increased exposure on your platforms. Emphasize the long-term value of the partnership and how it can lead to mutual growth.

6. Highlight your promotional plans: Clearly communicate your promotional strategies and plans for the affiliate program. Demonstrate how you intend to promote the products or services effectively, reaching a targeted audience and driving conversions. This can showcase your commitment and make the program more inclined to offer better terms.

7. Leverage multiple programs: If you have experience and success with multiple affiliate programs, use that as leverage. Inform the program you're negotiating with about your partnerships with their competitors and how your promotion can be redirected if a better deal is not reached.

8. Be prepared to negotiate: Enter negotiations with a clear understanding of your desired outcomes and alternatives if a deal cannot be reached. Be open to

compromise and flexible in your approach. Consider negotiating beyond just commissions, such as requesting higher payouts for specific products or exclusive bonuses for your audience.

9. Track and evaluate performance: Once you've secured a better commission or exclusive deal, continuously track and evaluate your performance. Provide regular reports to the affiliate program, demonstrating the value you deliver. This data can strengthen your position for future negotiations and potentially lead to further improvements.

Remember, negotiation is a process, and not all negotiations will end in your favor. Be persistent, professional, and adaptable in your approach.

CHAPTER SIX

Promoting Affiliate Products

Promoting affiliate products is a popular way for individuals and businesses to earn passive income online. Affiliate marketing involves promoting products or services created by other companies or individuals and earning a commission for each sale or action generated through your promotional efforts. Here is how to effectively promote affiliate products:

1. Choose a Niche: Select a niche or industry that aligns with your interests, knowledge, and target audience. It's crucial to choose a niche that has a demand for products and offers good earning potential.

2. Research Affiliate Programs: Look for reputable affiliate programs that offer products or services related to your chosen niche. Consider factors such as commission rates, product quality, affiliate support, and payment terms. Some popular affiliate networks include Amazon Associates, ClickBank, ShareASale, and Commission Junction.

3. Select Relevant Products: Once you've joined an affiliate program, browse through the available products and choose those that are relevant to your niche and will appeal to your audience. Focus on high-quality products that provide value to potential buyers.

4. Build a Website or Blog: Establish an online presence by creating a website or blog. This platform will serve as the foundation for promoting your affiliate products. Optimize your website for search engines (SEO) to increase its visibility and attract organic traffic.

5. Create High-Quality Content: Develop engaging and informative content that resonates with your target audience. This can include blog posts, articles, product reviews, tutorials, videos, and social media posts. Incorporate relevant affiliate links within your content naturally and transparently.

6. Drive Targeted Traffic: Implement various strategies to drive targeted traffic to your website. This can be achieved through SEO, social media marketing, email marketing, paid advertising, influencer collaborations, guest blogging, and participating in relevant online communities. The key is to reach out to your target audience and attract individuals who are genuinely interested in the products you promote.

7. Build an Email List: Encourage visitors to join your

email list by offering valuable incentives such as exclusive content, discounts, or freebies. Once you have a list of subscribers, you can regularly communicate with them, share relevant product recommendations, and promote affiliate offers through email marketing campaigns.

8. Utilize Social Media: Leverage social media platforms to expand your reach and engage with your audience. Create profiles on platforms where your target audience is active and share compelling content, including product recommendations. Use tracking links to monitor the performance of your social media promotions.

9. Establish Trust and Credibility: Build trust and credibility with your audience by providing honest and unbiased product reviews, demonstrating expertise in your niche, and offering valuable information. Avoid promoting products solely for the sake of earning commissions, as this can harm your reputation and credibility in the long run.

10. Track and Optimize: Monitor the performance of your affiliate promotions using analytics tools and affiliate tracking software. Track metrics such as click-through rates, conversion rates, and earnings to identify what's working and what needs improvement. Optimize your strategies based on the data you gather to

maximize your affiliate marketing efforts.

Remember, successful affiliate marketing requires time, effort, and persistence. Continuously educate yourself about industry trends, experiment with different promotional methods, and adapt your strategies to the evolving needs of your audience. By providing value and building genuine connections with your audience, you can create a sustainable and profitable affiliate marketing business.

Choosing the right affiliate products to promote

Choosing the right affiliate products to promote is crucial for the success of your affiliate marketing efforts. Here are some key factors to consider and a comprehensive explanation of each:

1. Relevance to Your Audience: The most important aspect is to select products that are relevant to your target audience. Consider their interests, needs, and preferences. By promoting products that align with their interests, you increase the likelihood of conversions and earning commissions. For example, if your website

focuses on fitness and health, promoting workout equipment or nutritional supplements would be appropriate.

2. Quality and Reputation: Ensure that the affiliate products you choose are of high quality and come from reputable brands. Your audience's trust is vital, and promoting subpar products can damage your credibility. Research the product, read reviews, and evaluate the reputation of the brand. Only promote products that you would genuinely recommend to others.

3. Commission Structure: Examine the commission structure offered by the affiliate program. Look for programs that provide competitive commission rates and favorable terms. Compare different affiliate programs to find the ones that offer a fair compensation for your promotional efforts.

4. Demand and Popularity: Consider the demand and popularity of the product. You want to promote products that have a significant market demand and a good track record of sales. Look for products that have positive trends and are likely to attract potential buyers. This can be determined by conducting market research, analyzing industry reports, or even observing the buzz around the product on social media platforms.

5. Competitive Advantage: Evaluate the product's

competitive advantage in the market. Determine what sets it apart from similar products and how it solves a problem or fulfills a need better than others. Products with unique features, superior quality, or innovative solutions tend to perform well and attract more buyers.

6. Affiliate Program Support: Assess the support provided by the affiliate program or the merchant. Look for programs that offer resources like marketing materials, tracking tools, and dedicated affiliate managers. Good support can make your promotional efforts more effective and streamline your affiliate marketing activities.

7. Longevity and Recurring Revenue: Consider whether the product offers recurring revenue opportunities or has the potential for repeat sales. Some affiliate programs provide commissions for recurring subscriptions or offer upsells and cross-sells, allowing you to earn commissions on subsequent purchases made by referred customers. These programs can provide a steady income stream over time.

8. Personal Experience and Expertise: Leverage your personal experience and expertise in selecting affiliate products. If you have firsthand knowledge of a product and can vouch for its quality and benefits, it can significantly enhance your promotional efforts. Your

genuine enthusiasm and authentic recommendations can resonate with your audience and lead to higher conversions.

Remember, the key is to strike a balance between promoting products that generate revenue and maintaining the trust and loyalty of your audience. By considering these factors and conducting thorough research, you can choose the right affiliate products that align with your audience's interests and meet their needs, while also maximizing your earning potential.

Crafting effective product reviews and recommendations

As an affiliate marketer, crafting effective product reviews and recommendations is crucial for driving sales and building trust with your audience. Here's a step-by-step guide on how to create compelling and comprehensive product reviews:

1. Select a Relevant Product: Choose a product that aligns with your niche and target audience. It's essential to review products you genuinely believe in and have

knowledge about.

2. Research the Product: Gather as much information as possible about the product. Read the product description, features, specifications, and any available user manuals. Also, explore customer reviews and ratings on various platforms to understand common feedback and concerns.

3. Use the Product Yourself (if possible): For an authentic review, try to get your hands on the product. Testing it allows you to provide personal insights, experiences, and real-life examples. If obtaining the product is not feasible, rely on extensive research and customer feedback.

4. Structure Your Review:

a. Introduction: Begin your review with an engaging introduction that captures the reader's attention. Clearly state the purpose of the review and the benefits the product offers.

b. Product Overview: Provide a concise overview of the product, including its name, brand, and key features. Mention any unique selling points or innovative aspects that differentiate it from competitors.

c. Benefits and Features: Highlight the specific benefits and features of the product. Explain how these features solve problems or meet the needs of your audience. Use bullet points or subheadings to make the information easy to scan and understand.

d. Pros and Cons: Present an honest evaluation of the product by discussing its strengths and weaknesses. Mention both positive and negative aspects, providing a balanced perspective. This helps establish credibility and builds trust with your audience.

e. Personal Experience (if applicable): Share your personal experience with the product, emphasizing how it has benefited you. Include specific details, anecdotes, and examples to make your review more relatable and persuasive.

f. Comparison to Competing Products: If there are similar products in the market, compare the reviewed product with its competitors. Highlight the advantages it has over other options and explain why it's the better choice.

g. Testimonials and Social Proof: Include snippets of customer testimonials or feedback to reinforce the product's value. If available, mention any endorsements or positive reviews from industry experts or influencers.

h. Call to Action: Encourage your readers to take action by providing a clear call to action. This could be a link to purchase the product, sign up for a free trial, or learn more information.

i. Disclosure: As an affiliate marketer, it's important to disclose your affiliate relationship with the product. This builds transparency and maintains trust with your audience.

5. Optimize for SEO: Use relevant keywords throughout your review to optimize it for search engines. Incorporate keywords naturally into your headings, subheadings, and body text. This helps improve your review's visibility and organic search traffic.

6. Be Honest and Transparent: Authenticity is key in building trust with your audience. Be transparent about your relationship with the product, and provide unbiased opinions. If the product has any drawbacks, mention them honestly. This integrity will strengthen your credibility and encourage long-term trust with your readers.

7. Use Visuals: Include high-quality images or videos of the product to enhance your review. Visuals can help readers visualize the product, understand its design, and get a better sense of its features.

8. Proofread and Edit: Before publishing your review, proofread it thoroughly to ensure clarity, accuracy, and proper grammar. Edit any sentences or paragraphs that may need improvement. A well-polished review demonstrates professionalism and attention to detail.

9. Promote Your Review: Once your review is published, promote it through

Using content marketing, email marketing, and social media to promote affiliate products

Content marketing, email marketing, and social media are powerful tools that can be used to promote affiliate products effectively. Let's explore each of these strategies and how they can be utilized to maximize your affiliate marketing efforts.

1. Content Marketing:

Content marketing involves creating and sharing valuable and relevant content to attract and engage your target audience. Here's how you can leverage content marketing to promote affiliate products:

a. Blogging: Start a blog where you can write informative and engaging articles related to the niche or industry of the affiliate products you're promoting. Provide valuable insights, tips, and advice to your readers. Within your blog posts, you can strategically place affiliate links to relevant products, making sure to disclose your affiliate relationship transparently.

b. Video Content: Create video content on platforms like YouTube or Vimeo, showcasing the features, benefits, and usage of the affiliate products. Demonstrate how the products solve a problem or enhance the lives of your viewers. Remember to include your affiliate links in the video descriptions or within the video itself, if applicable.

c. Guides and Tutorials: Develop comprehensive guides or tutorials related to the affiliate products. These can be in the form of ebooks, downloadable PDFs, or even online courses. Offer these resources as lead magnets on your website or blog, requiring visitors to provide their email addresses to access them. This leads us to the next strategy.

2. Email Marketing:

Email marketing is the process of using email to

communicate and build relationships with your audience. It's an effective way to promote affiliate products and nurture leads. Here's how you can utilize email marketing for affiliate promotion:

a. Building an Email List: Offer valuable content or incentives on your website or blog in exchange for visitors' email addresses. This allows you to build a targeted email list of potential customers interested in your niche. Use tools like opt-in forms, pop-ups, or landing pages to capture email addresses.

b. Segmenting Your Email List: Divide your email list into different segments based on various criteria such as interests, demographics, or purchase history. This allows you to send highly targeted and relevant emails to each segment, increasing the chances of conversions.

c. Email Sequences: Set up automated email sequences or drip campaigns that provide value, build trust, and subtly promote your affiliate products over time. Focus on educating your subscribers, solving their problems, and addressing their pain points. Incorporate affiliate links strategically within these emails, ensuring they are genuinely helpful to your subscribers.

3. Social Media:

Social media platforms provide a vast opportunity to

reach and engage with your target audience. Here's how you can leverage social media for affiliate marketing:

a. Choose the Right Platforms: Identify the social media platforms that align with your target audience. For example, if you're targeting professionals, LinkedIn might be more effective than Instagram.

b. Engage and Provide Value: Share valuable and relevant content related to your niche regularly. This can include blog posts, videos, infographics, or user-generated content. Engage with your followers by responding to comments, starting conversations, and addressing their questions or concerns.

c. Influencer Partnerships: Collaborate with influencers in your niche who have a significant following and credibility. They can promote your affiliate products to their audience through sponsored posts or affiliate links, driving more traffic and potential sales.

d. Paid Advertising: Consider running paid advertising campaigns on social media platforms. Platforms like Facebook, Instagram, or LinkedIn provide powerful targeting options that can help you reach a highly specific audience. Direct the traffic from these campaigns to your website or landing pages, where you can promote the affiliate products.

Remember, it's crucial to comply with relevant advertising and disclosure guidelines. Always disclose your affiliate relationship transparently to maintain trust with your audience.

Leveraging influencer marketing and partnerships

Leveraging influencer marketing and partnerships refers to the strategic use of influential individuals or popular content creators to promote a brand, product, or service to their audience. This marketing approach taps into the trust and credibility that these influencers have built with their followers, allowing brands to reach a wider audience and drive engagement.

Here is a comprehensive explanation of how influencer marketing and partnerships can be leveraged effectively:

1. Identify the Right Influencers: The first step is to identify influencers who align with your brand's values, target audience, and marketing goals. Consider factors such as their niche, follower demographics, engagement rates, and content quality. Look for influencers who have a genuine connection with their audience and can effectively communicate your brand message.

2. Set Clear Objectives: Define your marketing objectives and what you hope to achieve through influencer partnerships. This could be increasing brand awareness, driving website traffic, generating leads, boosting sales, or improving brand perception. Setting specific, measurable goals will help you evaluate the success of your influencer marketing campaigns.

3. Develop a Collaborative Strategy: Work closely with influencers to develop a collaborative strategy that aligns with both their content style and your brand's messaging. Provide them with guidelines, but also allow creative freedom to ensure authenticity and maintain their unique voice. This collaborative approach creates a win-win situation where influencers can create content that resonates with their audience while promoting your brand.

4. Content Creation and Distribution: Influencers can create various types of content, including sponsored posts, product reviews, tutorials, unboxing videos, giveaways, or brand collaborations. Encourage them to create engaging and authentic content that showcases your brand in a positive light. The content can be shared across multiple platforms such as social media, blogs, YouTube, or podcasts, depending on the influencers' primary channels.

5. Track and Measure Results: Implement a robust tracking system to measure the effectiveness of your influencer campaigns. Track metrics such as reach, engagement, website traffic, conversions, and sales attributed to the influencer partnerships. This data will help you assess the ROI of your campaigns and make informed decisions for future collaborations.

6. Long-term Partnerships: Consider building long-term relationships with influencers who consistently deliver positive results. Cultivating these partnerships can lead to deeper brand integrations, increased trust with their audience, and a more authentic representation of your brand. Long-term partnerships also allow influencers to become brand ambassadors, fostering stronger connections between the influencer, your brand, and their audience.

7. Compliance and Transparency: Ensure compliance with relevant advertising guidelines and regulations, such as disclosing sponsored content and adhering to ethical practices. Maintaining transparency and authenticity in influencer partnerships is crucial to building trust with both the influencer's audience and your own customers.

8. Monitor and Engage: Continuously monitor the performance of your influencer campaigns and actively

engage with the audience. Respond to comments, answer questions, and participate in discussions to foster a sense of community and strengthen your brand's presence. Influencer partnerships should be seen as an ongoing relationship rather than a one-time transaction.

By leveraging influencer marketing and partnerships effectively, brands can tap into the power of social influence, expand their reach, and build credibility with their target audience. It is a dynamic and ever-evolving strategy that requires careful planning, collaboration, and measurement to achieve desired results.

CHAPTER SEVEN

Tracking and Analytics

As an affiliate marketer, tracking and analytics are essential components of your success. They help you understand the performance of your marketing efforts, optimize your campaigns, and maximize your revenue. In this comprehensive explanation, I'll cover the key concepts and tools related to tracking and analytics in affiliate marketing.

1. Tracking:

Tracking involves monitoring and recording various data points related to your affiliate marketing campaigns. It allows you to track the actions of users, such as clicks, conversions, and sales, and attribute them to specific marketing activities. Here are some important tracking elements:

* Affiliate links: These are unique URLs provided by the affiliate network or program that you use. Each link contains a tracking code or ID that identifies you as the

affiliate. When users click on your affiliate link, the tracking code helps attribute their actions to your account.

* Cookies: Cookies are small text files stored on a user's device when they visit a website. In affiliate marketing, cookies play a crucial role in tracking. When someone clicks on your affiliate link, a cookie is placed on their device, allowing you to track their actions over a specific period (e.g., 30 days). If they make a purchase within that timeframe, you'll receive credit for the referral.

*SubIDs: SubIDs, also known as sub-parameters or sub-affiliate IDs, are additional tracking codes that you can add to your affiliate links. They help you identify the source of the traffic or specific marketing campaigns, enabling more granular tracking and analysis.

2. Analytics:

Analytics involves analyzing the tracked data to gain insights and make informed decisions. It allows you to measure the effectiveness of your marketing campaigns, understand user behavior, and optimize your strategies. Here are some important analytics aspects in affiliate marketing:

* Click-through rate (CTR): CTR measures the percentage of users who click on your affiliate link compared to the

total number of impressions or views. A higher CTR indicates better engagement and can help you assess the effectiveness of your promotional materials.

* Conversion rate: The conversion rate measures the percentage of users who complete a desired action, such as making a purchase, after clicking on your affiliate link. It's a crucial metric that indicates the quality of your traffic and the effectiveness of your pre-sale efforts.

* Earnings per click (EPC): EPC measures the average revenue generated per click on your affiliate link. It's calculated by dividing your total earnings by the number of clicks. EPC helps you assess the profitability of your campaigns and compare the performance of different affiliate offers.

* Return on investment (ROI): ROI measures the profitability of your marketing efforts. It compares the revenue you earn from your affiliate campaigns to the cost you incur (e.g., advertising costs). A positive ROI indicates a profitable campaign, while a negative ROI suggests the need for optimization.

3. Tracking and Analytics Tools:

To effectively track and analyze your affiliate marketing campaigns, you can leverage various tools and platforms. Here are some popular options:

* Affiliate networks: Many affiliate networks provide built-in tracking and analytics capabilities. They offer affiliate links with embedded tracking codes, real-time reporting dashboards, and detailed performance metrics.

* Third-party tracking platforms: You can use dedicated tracking platforms like Voluum, ClickMagick, or ThriveTracker. These tools offer advanced tracking features, customizable tracking links, conversion tracking, and detailed analytics to optimize your campaigns.

* Google Analytics: Google Analytics is a powerful web analytics tool that helps you track and analyze user behavior on your website. It can be integrated with your affiliate links to gain insights into the traffic, conversions, and other key metrics.

* UTM parameters: UTM parameters are tags added to your affiliate links to track the source, medium, and campaign name in Google Analytics or other analytics platforms. They provide additional data to analyze the performance of different marketing channels

Importance of tracking and analytics in affiliate marketing

Tracking and analytics play a crucial role in affiliate marketing, providing valuable insights and data that help optimize campaigns, measure performance, and make informed decisions. Here are the key reasons why tracking and analytics are important in affiliate marketing:

1. Performance Measurement: Tracking and analytics enable affiliates to measure the performance of their marketing efforts accurately. By implementing tracking pixels or codes on their websites or landing pages, affiliates can track various metrics such as clicks, conversions, sales, and revenue. This data allows them to evaluate the effectiveness of their campaigns, identify the best-performing channels, and make data-driven decisions to optimize their strategies.

2. Attribution and Commission Calculation: In affiliate marketing, multiple affiliates may contribute to a sale or conversion. Tracking and analytics help in accurately attributing each conversion to the appropriate affiliate. By using tracking software or platforms, affiliate marketers can assign unique identifiers or cookies to track customer journeys from the initial click to the final

conversion. This enables fair commission calculation and ensures affiliates are rewarded based on their actual contribution.

3. Optimization and ROI Improvement: Tracking and analytics provide valuable insights into campaign performance, allowing affiliates to identify areas for optimization. By analyzing data on clicks, conversions, and customer behavior, affiliates can determine which traffic sources, creatives, or offers are performing well and which are underperforming. This information helps them make data-driven decisions to optimize their campaigns, adjust targeting parameters, refine messaging, or test new strategies, ultimately improving return on investment (ROI).

4. Targeting and Segmentation: Tracking and analytics data can be used to segment and target specific audiences effectively. Affiliates can analyze customer data, such as demographics, interests, or purchasing behavior, to identify profitable segments and tailor their marketing messages accordingly. This enables them to deliver more personalized and relevant content, improving the chances of engaging potential customers and driving conversions.

5. Fraud Detection and Prevention: Tracking and analytics also play a crucial role in detecting and

preventing affiliate fraud. Affiliates can monitor their traffic patterns, conversion rates, and other relevant metrics to identify any suspicious or fraudulent activities, such as click fraud or cookie stuffing. By using sophisticated tracking systems and fraud detection tools, affiliates can take necessary measures to protect their campaigns and ensure the integrity of their affiliate marketing activities.

6. Relationship Management: For merchants or advertisers running affiliate programs, tracking and analytics provide valuable insights into their affiliate network's performance. They can track the performance of individual affiliates, analyze their traffic quality, and evaluate the return on investment generated by each affiliate. This data helps in managing relationships with affiliates, identifying top performers, and optimizing the program to attract and retain high-quality affiliates.

Tracking and analytics are essential in affiliate marketing as they enable performance measurement, accurate attribution, optimization, targeting, fraud detection, and effective relationship management. By leveraging the power of data and insights, affiliates and advertisers can maximize their ROI, improve campaign effectiveness, and drive sustainable growth in the competitive affiliate marketing landscape.

Implementing tracking systems and tools

As an affiliate marketer, implementing tracking systems and tools is crucial for measuring the success and effectiveness of your marketing campaigns. These tracking systems and tools allow you to track various metrics and gather data to optimize your campaigns, improve your conversions, and maximize your affiliate earnings. In this comprehensive explanation, I will outline the key steps and tools involved in implementing tracking systems as an affiliate marketer.

1. Define Your Tracking Goals: Start by identifying your tracking goals. What specific metrics do you want to measure? This could include clicks, conversions, sales, revenue, or any other relevant data points. Clearly defining your tracking goals will help you choose the right tracking tools and set up your tracking systems accordingly.

2. Choose a Tracking Platform: There are several tracking platforms available that cater specifically to affiliate marketers. Some popular options include Voluum, TrackingDesk, ThriveTracker, and ClickMagick. These

platforms offer advanced tracking features, reporting capabilities, and integrations with affiliate networks and traffic sources. Research and compare different platforms to find the one that best suits your needs and budget.

3. Set Up Tracking Links: Once you have chosen a tracking platform, you'll need to set up tracking links for your affiliate campaigns. These tracking links are unique URLs that redirect users to the merchant's website through your affiliate link. The tracking platform adds parameters to the URL to collect data and attribute conversions to your campaigns accurately. Most tracking platforms provide a user-friendly interface to generate tracking links quickly.

4. Integrate with Affiliate Networks: To track your affiliate campaigns effectively, you need to integrate your tracking platform with the affiliate networks you work with. This integration allows the tracking platform to receive real-time data about clicks, conversions, and other relevant information from the affiliate networks. Each tracking platform has its integration methods, such as API integration or post back URL setup. Follow the documentation or support resources provided by your tracking platform to establish the necessary integrations.

5. Implement Conversion Tracking: Conversion tracking is essential for measuring the success of your campaigns. It allows you to track when a user completes a desired action, such as making a purchase or signing up for a newsletter. Most affiliate networks provide a conversion tracking code or pixel that you can place on the merchant's thank-you page or confirmation page. This code fires when a conversion occurs, and the data is captured by your tracking platform.

6. Monitor and Analyze Data: With your tracking systems in place, regularly monitor and analyze the data provided by your tracking platform. Look for trends, patterns, and insights that can help you optimize your campaigns. Pay attention to conversion rates, click-through rates, traffic sources, and other relevant metrics. Identify high-performing campaigns and traffic sources, as well as areas that need improvement. Use this data to make data-driven decisions and refine your marketing strategies.

7. A/B Testing: A/B testing is a valuable technique in affiliate marketing. It involves testing different variations of your campaigns to identify the most effective elements. By split-testing different landing pages, ad creatives, headlines, or call-to-action buttons, you can determine what resonates best with your audience and drives higher conversions. Your tracking platform may

offer built-in A/B testing features, or you can use external tools like Optimizely or Google Optimize.

8. Optimize and Scale: Based on the insights gained from your tracking data and A/B testing optimize your campaigns to improve performance. Make adjustments to your targeting, messaging, or ad placements to maximize conversions and revenue. Once you have optimized your campaigns successfully, you can scale them by increasing your advertising budget, expanding into new traffic sources, or exploring additional affiliate networks.

Remember to comply with the tracking and privacy policies of the platforms you use, as well as any legal regulations related to data collection and user privacy. Additionally, stay up to date with industry

Interpreting key performance indicators (KPIs) and metrics

As an affiliate marketer, interpreting key performance indicators (KPIs) and metrics is essential for evaluating the success of your marketing efforts and making data-driven decisions. These metrics provide valuable insights into various aspects of your affiliate marketing campaigns and can help you optimize your strategies for better results. Let's go through some important KPIs and metrics in affiliate marketing and discuss their interpretation.

Click-Through Rate (CTR):

CTR is the percentage of people who click on your affiliate link or ad compared to the number of impressions it receives. A higher CTR indicates that your content or ad is compelling and attracts user interest. To improve CTR, you can focus on optimizing your ad copy, placement, and targeting.

Conversion Rate (CR):

Conversion rate measures the percentage of users who complete a desired action, such as making a purchase or signing up, after clicking on your affiliate link. A higher conversion rate indicates that your audience finds the offer appealing and relevant. To boost CR, you can improve the quality of your traffic, optimize landing pages, and ensure seamless user experience throughout the conversion process.

Earnings per Click (EPC):

EPC represents the average earnings you generate for

each click on your affiliate link. It's calculated by dividing the total earnings by the number of clicks. A higher EPC indicates that you're effectively monetizing your traffic and generating higher revenue. To increase EPC, you can focus on promoting high-converting offers, negotiating higher commissions, and refining your targeting to reach a more receptive audience.

Return on Investment (ROI):

ROI measures the profitability of your affiliate marketing campaigns. It's calculated by subtracting the cost of your campaign from the revenue generated and dividing it by the cost. A positive ROI indicates that your campaigns are generating profit, while a negative ROI suggests that adjustments are needed. To improve ROI, you can optimize your campaigns for higher conversion rates, reduce acquisition costs, and explore cost-effective advertising channels.

Average Order Value (AOV):

AOV represents the average amount spent by customers on each order generated through your affiliate links. A higher AOV means that your audience tends to make larger purchases, which can directly impact your earnings. To increase AOV, you can promote higher-priced products, upsell or cross-sell related products, and offer incentives for larger orders.

Traffic Sources:

Analyzing the sources of your traffic provides insights into the effectiveness of your marketing channels. By tracking the performance of different traffic sources, such as search engines, social media platforms, email campaigns, or specific websites, you can identify which sources are driving the most engaged users and adjust your marketing efforts accordingly. This helps you allocate your resources effectively and focus on the channels that deliver the best results.

Customer Lifetime Value (CLV):

CLV measures the total value a customer brings to your business over their lifetime as a customer. It considers factors such as repeat purchases, referrals, and upsells. By understanding CLV, you can assess the long-term profitability of your affiliate marketing efforts and make informed decisions about customer retention strategies, loyalty programs, and nurturing customer relationships.

Interpreting these KPIs and metrics collectively allows you to gain a comprehensive understanding of your affiliate marketing performance. It enables you to identify areas of improvement, optimize your campaigns, and make informed decisions to drive higher revenue and profitability. Regular monitoring and analysis of these metrics will help you stay on top of your affiliate marketing game and adapt to changing market dynamics.

Making data-driven decisions and optimizing performance

As an affiliate marketer, making data-driven decisions and optimizing performance is crucial for achieving success and maximizing your earnings. By leveraging data, you can gain valuable insights into your marketing campaigns, audience behavior, and conversion rates. This information allows you to make informed decisions and take targeted actions to improve your performance. Here's a comprehensive explanation of the process:

1. Define Key Performance Indicators (KPIs): Start by identifying the metrics that matter the most to your affiliate marketing business. These KPIs could include conversion rate, click-through rate, average order value, revenue per visitor, or return on investment (ROI). Clearly defining your KPIs will help you focus your efforts and measure your success.

2. Track and Analyze Data: Implement a robust tracking system to monitor the performance of your affiliate campaigns. This involves using tools such as Google Analytics, affiliate network tracking, or custom tracking solutions. Track important data points such as traffic sources, referral URLs, conversions, and revenue generated. Regularly analyze this data to uncover trends, patterns, and areas for improvement.

3. Split Testing and Experimentation: To optimize your performance, conduct split tests to compare different variables and determine which ones yield the best results. For example, you can test different landing page designs, call-to-action buttons, headlines, or promotional offers. Split testing helps you identify the most effective strategies and refine your marketing efforts accordingly.

4. Audience Segmentation: Divide your audience into different segments based on relevant characteristics such as demographics, interests, or behavior. This segmentation allows you to create personalized marketing campaigns tailored to specific groups. By targeting each segment with tailored content and offers, you can enhance engagement and conversion rates.

5. Affiliate Network Analysis: If you are working with multiple affiliate networks, analyze their performance

individually. Identify the networks that consistently generate high-quality traffic and conversions. Allocate more resources and focus on the networks that yield the best results while considering scaling down or discontinuing partnerships with underperforming networks.

6. Content Optimization: Regularly evaluate the performance of your content, whether its blog posts, product reviews, or email newsletters. Monitor engagement metrics like time on page, bounce rate, and social shares. Identify the type of content that resonates most with your audience and optimize it further to drive better results. This could involve improving headlines, enhancing readability, adding visuals, or incorporating strong calls-to-action.

7. Conversion Funnel Analysis: Analyze your conversion funnel to identify potential drop-off points or areas of friction that may hinder conversions. Examine each step of the funnel, from the initial ad impression to the final purchase, and pinpoint any bottlenecks or areas that need improvement. This analysis will help you optimize your funnel and increase conversion rates.

8. Affiliate Offer Selection: Continuously evaluate the performance of the affiliate offers you promote. Analyze the conversion rates, commission structures, product

quality, and customer feedback associated with each offer. Make data-driven decisions when selecting which offers to promote and focus on those that align with your audience's interests and have a track record of success.

9. Continuous Learning and Adaptation: Stay updated with the latest trends, techniques, and best practices in affiliate marketing. Attend industry conferences, join relevant communities, and follow authoritative blogs and podcasts. The affiliate marketing landscape is constantly evolving, so adaptability and continuous learning are essential for optimizing your performance.

By following these steps and leveraging data, you can make informed decisions to optimize your affiliate marketing performance. Remember that data-driven decision-making is an iterative process, and it's important to regularly monitor and analyze your data to stay ahead of the competition and achieve long-term success.

CHAPTER EIGHT

Scaling and Diversifying Affiliate Income

Scaling and diversifying affiliate income refers to the process of increasing and expanding your earnings as an affiliate marketer by utilizing various strategies and sources of revenue. Instead of relying on a single affiliate program or product, you aim to broaden your income streams and reach a wider audience. Here's a comprehensive explanation of how you can achieve this:

1. Identify your niche: Start by identifying your niche or target market. This allows you to focus your efforts on a specific audience and tailor your affiliate promotions accordingly. By understanding the needs and interests of your niche, you can provide more valuable content and recommendations to your audience.

2. Build a content-rich website or blog: Establishing a website or blog is crucial for scaling and diversifying your affiliate income. Create high-quality, informative, and engaging content related to your niche. This content can

include product reviews, tutorials, guides, comparisons, and any other relevant information that adds value to your readers. As your website gains authority and attracts more traffic, you can leverage this to promote various affiliate products and services.

3. Join multiple affiliate programs: Instead of relying solely on one affiliate program, consider joining multiple programs that align with your niche. This allows you to diversify your income streams and gives you access to a wider range of products or services to promote. Look for reputable affiliate networks or platforms that offer a variety of affiliate programs, or reach out to individual companies within your niche to inquire about their affiliate opportunities.

4. Promote relevant and high-converting products: Select affiliate products or services that are relevant to your niche and have a proven track record of conversions. Focus on promoting quality products that you genuinely believe in, as this builds trust with your audience. By recommending valuable products, you increase the likelihood of earning commissions and retaining your audience's trust in the long run.

5. Incorporate different types of affiliate promotions: Explore various types of affiliate promotions to diversify your income. These can include banner ads, text links,

product reviews, sponsored content, email marketing, social media campaigns, webinars, and more. Experiment with different approaches to find what works best for your audience and yields the highest conversions.

6. Implement SEO strategies: Search Engine Optimization (SEO) plays a crucial role in scaling your affiliate income. Optimize your website's content and structure to improve its visibility on search engines. By targeting relevant keywords, optimizing Meta tags, improving site speed, and acquiring backlinks from reputable sources, you can attract organic traffic and increase your chances of earning affiliate commissions.

7. Explore additional monetization methods: In addition to affiliate marketing, consider exploring other monetization methods to further diversify your income. This can include display advertising, sponsored content, selling digital products (e.g., e-books, online courses), offering consulting services, or creating a membership site. By incorporating multiple revenue streams, you become less dependent on a single source of income.

8. Leverage email marketing: Build an email list by offering valuable content or incentives to your audience. By nurturing your email subscribers, you can cultivate a loyal following and increase the likelihood of affiliate

sales. Regularly send out newsletters, exclusive promotions, or personalized recommendations to your email list, ensuring that your subscribers remain engaged and receptive to your affiliate offers.

9. Analyze data and optimize performance: Continuously monitor and analyze your affiliate marketing efforts. Track key performance indicators (KPIs) such as click-through rates, conversion rates, and earnings per click. Identify top-performing affiliate products, optimize underperforming campaigns, and adapt your strategies based on the data you gather. This iterative approach allows you to refine your tactics and maximize your earning potential.

10. Stay up-to-date and adapt: The affiliate marketing landscape is constantly evolving. Stay informed about industry trends, new products, and emerging technologies that can enhance your affiliate marketing efforts

Strategies for scaling affiliate marketing efforts

Scaling affiliate marketing efforts involves expanding and optimizing your affiliate program to increase the number of affiliates, drive more traffic, and generate higher conversions. Here are some strategies to help you scale your affiliate marketing efforts:

1. Establish Clear Objectives: Clearly define your goals and objectives for scaling your affiliate program. Determine what metrics you want to improve, such as the number of affiliates, traffic, conversions, or revenue. This will guide your strategies and help you measure success.

2. Recruit and Engage Quality Affiliates: Focus on recruiting affiliates who align with your target audience and have relevant content or a large following. Reach out to influencers, bloggers, content creators, and industry experts. Offer them competitive commission rates, incentives, and exclusive promotions to motivate them to join and promote your products or services.

3. Optimize Commission Structure: Review your commission structure to ensure it is competitive and attractive to potential affiliates. Consider offering tiered commissions or performance-based incentives to encourage affiliates to drive more sales or leads. Test different commission rates to find the optimal balance between profitability and motivating affiliates.

4. Provide Promotional Materials: Offer a variety of promotional materials such as banners, product images,

text links, and sample content. Make it easy for affiliates to access and use these materials on their websites, blogs, or social media platforms. Personalize the materials to match each affiliate's brand and audience.

5. Offer Affiliate Training and Support: Provide training materials, guides, and webinars to educate your affiliates on your products or services, affiliate marketing strategies, and best practices. Offer ongoing support through email, chat, or a dedicated affiliate manager who can assist with queries, offer guidance, and address concerns.

6. Track and Optimize Performance: Use robust affiliate tracking software to monitor affiliate performance, track clicks, conversions, and sales. Analyze data to identify top-performing affiliates, high-converting traffic sources, and successful promotional strategies. Optimize your program based on these insights, focusing on rewarding and replicating what works best.

7. Leverage Technology and Automation: Utilize affiliate marketing tools and platforms to streamline your program. These tools can automate processes such as affiliate recruitment, tracking, payouts, and reporting. Automation frees up time and resources, allowing you to focus on strategic growth and relationship building.

8. Nurture Relationships with Affiliates: Cultivate strong

relationships with your affiliates by providing regular communication, updates, and exclusive offers. Recognize and reward top-performing affiliates, and consider collaborating on content, events, or joint promotions. Building strong partnerships encourages loyalty and motivates affiliates to invest more effort in promoting your brand.

9. Expand Affiliate Network: Explore opportunities to expand your affiliate network beyond traditional bloggers and influencers. Consider partnering with complementary businesses, industry associations, or affiliate networks to tap into new audiences and markets. These partnerships can provide access to a wider pool of potential affiliates and increase your brand exposure.

10. Continuously Test and Iterate: Keep testing new strategies, promotional techniques, commission structures, and affiliate incentives. Continuously analyze data and metrics to identify areas for improvement. Adapt and refine your strategies based on performance insights, industry trends, and feedback from affiliates.

Remember, scaling affiliate marketing efforts takes time and requires consistent effort. By implementing these strategies and continuously optimizing your program, you can effectively grow your affiliate network, increase traffic, and drive higher conversions for your business.

Expanding into new markets and niches

Expanding into new markets and niches as an affiliate marketer can be a strategic move to diversify your income streams and reach a broader audience. Here's a comprehensive explanation of how you can approach this expansion:

1. Market Research: Start by conducting thorough market research to identify potential new markets and niches that align with your existing expertise and interests. Look for markets with growing demand, untapped opportunities, and a target audience that could benefit from your affiliate products or services.

2. Identify Target Audience: Once you've chosen a new market or niche, identify your target audience within that segment. Understand their needs, preferences, pain points, and buying behaviors. This information will help you tailor your marketing efforts and select the most relevant affiliate products or services to promote.

3. Evaluate Competition: Assess the competition in the

new market or niche. Identify other affiliate marketers or businesses targeting the same audience. Analyze their strategies, offerings, and content to find gaps or areas where you can differentiate yourself and provide unique value.

4. Choose Affiliate Programs: Research and select affiliate programs that offer products or services relevant to your new target audience. Look for reputable programs with attractive commission structures, reliable tracking systems, and quality products or services. Consider reaching out to potential affiliate partners directly to negotiate better terms or exclusivity.

5. Create Targeted Content: Develop high-quality content that resonates with your new target audience. This can include blog posts, articles, videos, podcasts, social media content, or email newsletters. Provide valuable information, address their pain points, and demonstrate how the affiliate products or services can solve their problems or enhance their lives.

6. Optimize SEO: Implement search engine optimization (SEO) strategies to increase your visibility in search engine results for relevant keywords in your new market or niche. Conduct keyword research to identify the most relevant and frequently searched terms. Optimize your content, meta tags, headers, and URLs accordingly to

improve your organic search rankings.

7. Leverage Social Media: Utilize social media platforms to connect with your new target audience. Identify the platforms they are most active on and create engaging content tailored to each platform. Build a community, engage with your audience, and share valuable insights or promotions related to your affiliate products or services.

8. Collaborate and Network: Establish relationships with influencers, bloggers, or content creators in your new market or niche. Collaborate on joint ventures, guest posts, or affiliate partnerships to tap into their existing audience and expand your reach. Networking with industry experts and attending relevant events can also help you build credibility and identify new opportunities.

9. Track and Analyze Results: Monitor the performance of your affiliate marketing efforts in the new market or niche. Use tracking tools and analytics to measure the effectiveness of your campaigns, conversion rates, and revenue generated. Identify areas for improvement, make data-driven decisions, and optimize your strategies accordingly.

10. Adapt and Evolve: As you expand into new markets and niches, be prepared to adapt and evolve your approach. Stay updated with industry trends, consumer

preferences, and changes in the affiliate marketing landscape. Continuously refine your strategies, experiment with new tactics, and stay committed to providing value to your target audience.

Remember that expanding into new markets and niches requires time, effort, and a willingness to learn. Be patient, persistent, and adaptable as you navigate the challenges and opportunities that come with diversifying your affiliate marketing business.

Creating multiple income streams through diversification

Diversification is a key strategy for creating multiple income streams as an affiliate marketer. By diversifying your income sources, you can reduce risk, increase your earning potential, and adapt to changes in the market. Here's a comprehensive explanation of how you can achieve diversification as an affiliate marketer:

1. Choose Multiple Affiliate Programs: Instead of relying solely on one affiliate program, join multiple programs that align with your niche or target audience. This allows

you to promote a variety of products or services and earn commissions from different sources. Look for reputable programs with competitive commission rates and a wide range of offerings.

2. Promote Different Product Types: Within your chosen affiliate programs, diversify the types of products or services you promote. For example, if you're promoting fitness products, you could promote workout equipment, supplements, fitness apparel, and online training programs. This way, you can cater to various customer preferences and increase your earning potential.

3. Explore Different Marketing Channels: Instead of relying solely on one marketing channel, such as a blog or social media platform, diversify your marketing efforts across multiple channels. This could include creating a YouTube channel, starting a podcast, or engaging with your audience through email marketing. By diversifying your channels, you can reach a wider audience and attract different types of customers.

4. Create Your Own Products or Services: As an affiliate marketer, you can also create your own products or services to sell alongside affiliate offers. For example, you could develop an e-book, an online course, or offer consulting services in your niche. This way, you have

control over your pricing and can earn higher profits compared to affiliate commissions alone.

5. Build an Email List: Building an email list is an effective way to diversify your income streams. By collecting email addresses from your website visitors or social media followers, you can nurture a relationship with your audience and promote affiliate offers or your own products directly to them. An engaged and responsive email list can become a valuable asset and a consistent source of income.

6. Explore Passive Income Opportunities: Look for affiliate programs or opportunities that offer passive income streams. These could include recurring commissions for subscription-based products or services, such as membership sites or software subscriptions. By promoting such programs, you can earn ongoing commissions as long as your referrals remain customers.

7. Consider High-Ticket Affiliate Programs: In addition to promoting low-cost affiliate products, consider partnering with high-ticket affiliate programs. These programs offer products or services with higher price points, resulting in larger commission payouts. While high-ticket sales may require more effort to convert, a single successful sale can significantly boost your

income.

8. Expand Your Target Audience: If you've been focusing on a specific niche, consider expanding your target audience to reach a broader market. This could involve exploring related niches or targeting different demographics within your niche. By expanding your audience, you can tap into new income streams and attract a wider range of customers.

9. Stay Updated and Adapt: The affiliate marketing landscape is constantly evolving, so it's essential to stay updated with industry trends and adapt your strategies accordingly. Keep an eye on emerging affiliate programs, changing consumer behaviors, and new marketing techniques. This flexibility will help you identify new income opportunities and stay ahead of the competition.

Remember, building multiple income streams takes time and effort. It's crucial to maintain consistency, provide value to your audience, and continuously refine your strategies to maximize your earning potential as an affiliate marketer.

Exploring advanced techniques such as funnel optimization and retargeting

As an affiliate marketer, implementing advanced techniques like funnel optimization and retargeting can significantly improve your conversion rates and overall success. These strategies focus on maximizing the value of each visitor by guiding them through a well-designed funnel and engaging them with personalized content. Here's an overview of these techniques:

Funnel Optimization:

Funnel optimization involves creating a structured sequence of steps that lead your visitors from initial awareness to making a purchase. Here are some key steps to consider:

a. Targeted Traffic: Ensure you're driving targeted traffic to your funnel by using methods like search engine optimization (SEO), pay-per-click (PPC) advertising, social media marketing, or email marketing. This helps attract visitors who are genuinely interested in your affiliate offers.

b. Captivating Landing Page: Create an enticing landing

page that grabs visitors' attention, highlights the benefits of the product or service you're promoting, and encourage them to take the desired action (e.g., signing up or making a purchase). A clear call-to-action (CTA) is crucial.

c. Email Capture: Implement email capture mechanisms, such as opt-in forms or lead magnets, to collect visitors' email addresses. This allows you to continue engaging with them through email marketing and build a long-term relationship.

d. Follow-up Sequences: Develop automated email sequences that nurture leads and provide valuable content related to the affiliate offer. Gradually introduce the benefits of the product or service and address any concerns or objections.

e. Upsells and Downsells: Consider offering relevant upsells or downsells during the checkout process. This can help increase the average order value and maximize your affiliate commissions.

Retargeting:

Retargeting involves showing personalized ads to people who have previously visited your website or engaged with your content. It helps you stay top-of-mind and increases the chances of conversion. Here's how you can leverage retargeting:

a. Pixel Implementation: Install retargeting pixels or tags provided by advertising platforms like Facebook, Google, or LinkedIn on your website. These pixels track visitors and enable you to retarget them with ads.

b. Custom Audience Creation: Segment your audience based on their behavior on your website. For example, you can create a custom audience of people who added products to the cart but didn't complete the purchase.

c. Ad Campaigns: Create targeted ad campaigns using platforms like Facebook Ads or Google Ads, specifically tailored to your custom audiences. Craft compelling ad copies and visuals that remind visitors of the product or service they showed interest in.

d. Dynamic Product Ads: Utilize dynamic product ads to display ads featuring the exact products or services visitors viewed on your website. This level of personalization can significantly increase the chances of conversion.

e. Test and Refine: Continuously monitor and analyze the performance of your retargeting campaigns. Experiment with different ad formats, placements, and audience segments to optimize your results over time.

Remember to comply with relevant privacy regulations

and ensure you have visitors' consent for using their data in retargeting campaigns.

By implementing funnel optimization techniques and leveraging retargeting strategies, you can enhance your affiliate marketing efforts, increase conversions, and maximize your overall revenue.

CHAPTER NINE

Building Relationships and Networking

As an affiliate marketer, building relationships and networking are crucial for your success. Here are some tips to help you build strong relationships and expand your network:

1. Identify your target audience: Understand who your target audience is and what they are interested in. This will help you connect with like-minded individuals and businesses.

2. Engage in online communities: Join relevant online communities such as forums, social media groups, and industry-specific websites. Participate actively by providing valuable insights, answering questions, and sharing your expertise.

3. Attend industry events: Attend conferences, seminars, and trade shows related to your niche. These events provide excellent networking opportunities where you

can meet industry experts, potential partners, and other affiliate marketers.

4. Create valuable content: Produce high-quality content that offers value to your target audience. This could include blog posts, videos, podcasts, or social media updates. By consistently providing valuable content, you can attract and engage with your audience, building trust and credibility.

5. Collaborate with influencers and bloggers: Reach out to influencers and bloggers in your niche and propose collaborations. This could involve guest posting on their blogs, collaborating on social media campaigns, or creating joint webinars or podcasts. Such collaborations can help you tap into their audience and expand your reach.

6. Leverage social media platforms: Utilize social media platforms like LinkedIn, Twitter, and Facebook to connect with industry professionals, potential partners, and customers. Engage in conversations, share valuable content, and build relationships through direct messaging.

7. Offer affiliate partnerships: Identify complementary products or services in your niche and reach out to the businesses offering them. Propose an affiliate partnership where you promote their products or

services and earn a commission for each sale referred through your affiliate links. Building these partnerships can expand your network and create mutually beneficial relationships.

8. Attend local business events: Don't limit yourself to online networking. Explore local business events, meet ups, or workshops in your area. These events allow you to connect with professionals from various industries and potentially find collaborations or partnerships.

9. Nurture existing relationships: Building relationships is not just about making new connections; it's also about nurturing existing ones. Stay in touch with your contacts, engage with their content, and offer support whenever possible. Building strong, long-term relationships can lead to referrals and collaborations in the future.

Remember, building relationships and networking take time and effort. Be genuine, provide value, and focus on building mutually beneficial relationships.

Importance of building relationships with affiliate managers and industry professionals

Building relationships with affiliate managers and industry professionals is crucial for several reasons:

1. Collaboration and Partnership: Affiliate marketing thrives on collaboration and partnerships. By developing relationships with affiliate managers and industry professionals, you can establish mutually beneficial partnerships. This collaboration can lead to access to exclusive offers, higher commission rates, and special promotions that can enhance your earning potential as an affiliate marketer.

2. Insider Knowledge and Insights: Affiliate managers and industry professionals possess valuable knowledge and insights about the industry. They are well-versed in the latest trends, strategies, and best practices. By cultivating relationships with them, you can gain access to this insider knowledge, stay updated on industry developments, and leverage their expertise to improve your own marketing efforts.

3. Networking Opportunities: Building relationships within the affiliate marketing industry expands your professional network. Networking with affiliate managers and industry professionals can lead to new opportunities, such as joint ventures, guest blogging, podcast interviews, or speaking engagements. These connections can help you enhance your visibility and credibility within the industry, opening doors to further growth and success.

4. Support and Guidance: Affiliate managers are there to support you and help you succeed. By establishing relationships with them, you gain access to their guidance and support whenever you encounter challenges or have questions. They can provide you with advice, troubleshooting tips, and personalized strategies to optimize your affiliate campaigns. Having a strong support system within the industry can significantly accelerate your learning curve and overall progress.

5. Trust and Reputation: Building relationships with affiliate managers and industry professionals can enhance your trustworthiness and reputation as an affiliate marketer. When you establish strong relationships, you demonstrate your commitment to professionalism and collaboration. This can lead to recommendations and referrals from industry experts, which in turn can attract more affiliate opportunities

and establish you as a trusted authority within the industry.

6. Early Access and Exclusive Opportunities: Affiliate managers often have access to new products, services, or promotions before they are widely released. By building relationships with them, you may gain early access to these opportunities, allowing you to be among the first to promote them. This can give you a competitive edge, as you can capture the attention of your audience with fresh and exclusive offers.

Building relationships with affiliate managers and industry professionals is essential for collaboration, access to insider knowledge, networking, support, trust building, and gaining exclusive opportunities. These relationships can significantly contribute to your success as an affiliate marketer by providing you with valuable resources, guidance, and growth opportunities within the industry.

Participating in affiliate marketing events and conferences

Participating in affiliate marketing events and conferences can be a valuable opportunity for affiliate marketers to network, gain insights, and stay up to date with industry trends. These events bring together professionals, experts, and companies in the affiliate marketing space, providing a platform for learning, collaboration, and business development. Here's a comprehensive explanation of participating in affiliate marketing events and conferences:

1. Networking: Affiliate marketing events and conferences offer excellent networking opportunities. You can meet industry leaders, fellow affiliates, advertisers, affiliate networks, and service providers. Building relationships with these individuals can lead to partnerships, collaborations, and future business opportunities.

2. Knowledge sharing: Events and conferences feature presentations, panel discussions, workshops, and keynote speeches by industry experts. These sessions cover various topics such as affiliate marketing

strategies, optimization techniques, emerging trends, legal and regulatory updates, and case studies. Attending these sessions can provide you with valuable insights and knowledge to enhance your affiliate marketing efforts.

3. Industry trends and updates: Affiliate marketing events and conferences often showcase the latest trends, technologies, and best practices in the industry. You can learn about new affiliate programs, innovative marketing techniques, conversion optimization strategies, and emerging niches. Staying updated with industry trends can help you stay competitive and adapt your marketing strategies accordingly.

4. Product and service discovery: Many events and conferences have an exhibition area where companies showcase their products, services, and affiliate programs. This provides an opportunity to discover new affiliate offers, explore potential partnerships, and learn about the latest tools and technologies that can enhance your affiliate marketing campaigns.

5. Professional development: Participating in affiliate marketing events and conferences can contribute to your professional development. By attending sessions, workshops, and master classes, you can enhance your skills, gain new perspectives, and stay ahead of the

curve. Some events even offer certifications or continuing education credits, which can add value to your professional profile.

6. Building your personal brand: Events and conferences allow you to establish yourself as an authority and thought leader in the affiliate marketing space. By actively participating in discussions, speaking on panels, or delivering presentations, you can showcase your expertise and gain recognition within the industry. This can lead to new business opportunities, partnerships, and speaking engagements in the future.

7. Industry connections: Affiliate marketing events and conferences attract a diverse group of professionals from various sectors of the industry. Building connections with affiliate networks, advertisers, publishers, and service providers can be beneficial for your business. These connections can lead to potential collaborations, exclusive offers, and access to valuable resources.

8. Motivation and inspiration: Immersing yourself in an environment of like-minded professionals and industry experts can be motivating and inspiring. Hearing success stories, learning from others' experiences, and being surrounded by individuals who share your passion for affiliate marketing can reignite your enthusiasm and

drive for your own projects.

To make the most of affiliate marketing events and conferences, it's essential to plan ahead, set goals, and actively engage during the event. Prioritize sessions and activities that align with your interests and objectives, and make sure to network and build relationships with other attendees. Follow up with the connections you make after the event to maintain those relationships and explore potential collaborations.

Overall, participating in affiliate marketing events and conferences can provide immense value to affiliate marketers, offering opportunities for networking, learning, and business growth. It's a chance to stay updated, gain insights, and connect with industry professionals, all of which can contribute to your success in the field of affiliate marketing.

Collaborating with other affiliates and influencers

Collaborating with other affiliates and influencers can be a highly effective strategy for expanding your reach, increasing brand awareness, and driving more conversions. When done correctly, it can create a mutually beneficial partnership that leverages the audiences and expertise of both parties. Here's a comprehensive explanation of how collaborating with affiliates and influencers can work:

1. Understanding Affiliates and Influencers:

* Affiliates: Affiliates are individuals or companies who promote your products or services in exchange for a commission on each sale they generate. They typically have their own websites, blogs, or social media channels where they share their affiliate links.

* Influencers: Influencers are individuals with a significant online following and the ability to impact the purchasing decisions of their audience. They can be found on various platforms such as social media, blogs, YouTube, or podcasts.

2. Finding the Right Partners:

* Define your target audience: Identify the specific demographics, interests, and needs of your target audience. This will help you find affiliates and influencers whose followers align with your target market.

* Research potential partners: Look for affiliates and

influencers who have an engaged audience, a good reputation, and content that complements your brand. Consider factors like follower count, engagement rate, content quality, and audience demographics.

3. Negotiating the Partnership:

* Commission structure: Determine the commission or compensation structure that works for both parties. It can be a percentage of sales, a flat fee, or a combination of both.

* Collaboration terms: Clearly outline the expectations, responsibilities, and deliverables of each party. This may include content creation, promotion schedules, exclusivity agreements, and campaign duration.

4. Implementing the Collaboration:

* Affiliate tracking: Provide affiliates with unique tracking links or promo codes to attribute sales to their efforts. This allows you to accurately measure their performance and calculate commissions.

* Collaborative content: Work with influencers to create engaging content that highlights your products or services. This can include sponsored posts, reviews, tutorials, giveaways, or endorsements.

* Cross-promotion: Encourage affiliates and influencers

to promote each other's content to maximize exposure and reach new audiences. This can involve sharing social media posts, guest blogging, or co-hosting events.

5. Monitoring and Optimizing:

* Performance tracking: Regularly monitor the performance of your affiliates and influencers. Track key metrics such as clicks, conversions, revenue generated, and engagement levels to assess the success of the collaboration.

* Providing support: Offer ongoing support to your partners by answering their questions, providing marketing materials, or addressing any issues they may encounter.

* Optimizing strategies: Continuously analyze the data and feedback to optimize your collaboration strategies. Experiment with different approaches, partnerships, and promotional tactics to improve results over time.

Remember, successful collaborations with affiliates and influencers require clear communication, mutual trust, and a shared vision. By strategically selecting partners and implementing effective collaboration techniques, you can harness the power of these relationships to expand your brand's reach and drive business growth.

Leveraging networking opportunities for growth and partnerships

As an affiliate marketer, networking opportunities can play a crucial role in your growth and success. Building strong partnerships and connections within your industry can open up a world of possibilities for expanding your reach, increasing your revenue, and accessing valuable resources. Here's a comprehensive explanation of how you can leverage networking opportunities for growth and partnerships as an affiliate marketer:

1. Expand your professional network: Networking allows you to connect with like-minded individuals, industry experts, and potential partners. Attend relevant conferences, seminars, and trade shows where you can meet affiliate managers, advertisers, and fellow marketers. Engage in conversations, exchange contact information, and build relationships with people who can contribute to your growth.

2. Seek out affiliate networks: Joining affiliate networks can provide you with a platform to connect with a wide range of advertisers and affiliate managers. These

networks act as intermediaries, facilitating partnerships between affiliates and advertisers. By joining reputable affiliate networks, you gain access to a pool of potential partners and a variety of affiliate programs to promote.

3. Participate in industry forums and communities: Engaging in online forums and communities focused on affiliate marketing allows you to interact with experienced affiliates, ask questions, and learn from others' experiences. It's an excellent opportunity to showcase your expertise, establish yourself as a trusted affiliate marketer, and connect with potential partners or clients who may be browsing these platforms.

4. Build relationships with affiliate managers: Affiliate managers are pivotal in establishing successful partnerships with advertisers. They can provide valuable insights, promotional materials, exclusive offers, and higher commissions. By networking with affiliate managers, you can develop stronger connections, negotiate better deals, and gain access to valuable resources that can boost your marketing efforts.

5. Collaborate with complementary affiliates: Look for affiliates who have complementary products or services to your own. Collaborating with these affiliates can lead to mutually beneficial partnerships, such as cross-promotions or joint ventures. By leveraging each other's

audiences and sharing resources, you can reach a wider customer base and increase your overall conversions.

6. Attend industry events and conferences: Industry events and conferences offer excellent networking opportunities. These gatherings bring together professionals from various sectors, including advertisers, publishers, and industry influencers. By attending, you can meet potential partners, establish new relationships, and stay updated on the latest trends and innovations in the affiliate marketing industry.

7. Be active on social media: Utilize social media platforms, such as LinkedIn, Twitter, and Facebook, to connect with industry professionals, join relevant groups, and participate in discussions. Share valuable content, provide insights, and engage with others to build your personal brand and expand your network. Social media can also be a platform for direct communication with potential partners or clients.

8. Offer value and be genuine: When networking, focus on providing value to others rather than solely promoting your own products or services. Offer your expertise, share insights, and help others solve problems. By being genuine, helpful, and approachable, you can establish trust and credibility within your network, making it more likely for potential partners to

want to collaborate with you.

9. Follow up and nurture relationships: Building a network is not just about making initial connections; it's also about nurturing and maintaining relationships over time. Follow up with the contacts you make, send personalized messages, and stay engaged by sharing relevant information or congratulating them on their achievements. Regularly nurturing your relationships will strengthen your network and increase the likelihood of future collaborations.

Remember, networking is a long-term strategy that requires consistent effort and dedication. By leveraging networking opportunities, you can tap into a vast pool of knowledge, resources, and potential partnerships, which can significantly contribute to your growth and success as an affiliate marketer.

CHAPTER TEN

Overcoming Challenges and Staying Motivated

As an affiliate marketer, you may encounter various challenges along your journey. However, with the right mindset and strategies, you can overcome these challenges and stay motivated to achieve your goals. Here are some key points to help you navigate the affiliate marketing landscape:

1. Set Clear Goals: Start by setting specific, measurable, achievable, relevant, and time-bound (SMART) goals. Having a clear direction will keep you focused and motivated. Break down your goals into smaller milestones, which can provide a sense of achievement as you progress.

2. Choose the Right Niche: Select a niche that aligns with your interests, expertise, and market demand. Working in a niche you are passionate about will make it easier to stay motivated and create valuable content for your

audience.

3. Build a Strong Foundation: Invest time in building a solid foundation for your affiliate marketing business. This includes creating a professional website or blog, optimizing it for search engines, and establishing a strong online presence through social media channels. A well-designed and user-friendly platform will attract more visitors and enhance your credibility.

4. High-Quality Content Creation: Focus on producing high-quality, valuable content that resonates with your target audience. Provide informative articles, tutorials, reviews, and other relevant content that helps solve their problems or addresses their needs. Engage with your audience through comments, emails, or social media to build relationships and establish trust.

5. SEO and Traffic Generation: Learn the basics of search engine optimization (SEO) to improve your website's visibility in search engine results. Target relevant keywords in your content, optimize meta tags, and build backlinks from reputable sources. Additionally, explore other traffic generation methods such as social media marketing, guest blogging, and email marketing to diversify your traffic sources.

6. Choose Reliable Affiliate Programs: Research and select reputable affiliate programs that offer products or

services relevant to your niche. Look for programs with fair commission structures, accurate tracking systems, and good support. Partnering with trustworthy brands adds credibility to your recommendations and increases the likelihood of conversions.

7. Track and Analyze Results: Regularly track and analyze your affiliate marketing efforts to identify what's working and what's not. Monitor metrics like traffic, click-through rates, conversions, and revenue generated. This data will help you optimize your strategies, focus on high-performing channels, and make informed decisions to improve your results.

8. Stay Updated and Adapt: The affiliate marketing landscape is constantly evolving, with new technologies, trends, and strategies emerging. Stay updated with industry news, attend webinars, read relevant blogs, and join communities to network with other affiliate marketers. Adapt to changes by incorporating new techniques, tools, or platforms that can enhance your marketing efforts.

9. Seek Support and Collaboration: Affiliate marketing can sometimes feel isolating, so it's crucial to seek support from like-minded individuals. Join online forums or communities where you can connect with fellow marketers, share experiences, and learn from one

another. Collaborating with others on projects or joint ventures can also provide fresh perspectives and keep you motivated.

10. Stay Positive and Persistent: Affiliate marketing success doesn't happen overnight. It requires consistent effort, patience, and resilience. Stay positive, celebrate small victories, and learn from any setbacks you encounter. Maintain a long-term mindset and remind yourself of your goals and the reasons why you embarked on this journey in the first place.

By following these strategies and maintaining a strong work ethic, you can overcome challenges, stay motivated, and build a successful affiliate marketing business. Remember, it's a continuous learning process, so keep exploring new opportunities and refining your strategies along the way.

Common challenges faced by affiliate marketers and how to overcome them

Affiliate marketing can be a lucrative venture, but like any business, it comes with its own set of challenges.

Understanding and addressing these challenges is crucial for success in the field. Here are some common challenges faced by affiliate marketers and strategies to overcome them:

1. Finding Profitable Niches: Identifying a profitable niche can be challenging. It requires thorough market research and analysis to determine which niches have high demand and low competition. To overcome this challenge, conduct keyword research, analyze trends, and explore affiliate networks and marketplaces to find niches with potential. Look for niches where you have a genuine interest or expertise, as it will make your marketing efforts more effective.

2. Building an Audience: Affiliate marketers rely on attracting and engaging a targeted audience to promote products or services effectively. Building an audience takes time and effort, especially in today's competitive digital landscape. Create a content strategy that focuses on providing value to your audience through blog posts, videos, social media, or podcasts. Use SEO techniques to increase your visibility in search engine results. Engage with your audience through comments, emails, and social media interactions to build trust and loyalty.

3. Generating Quality Traffic: Driving traffic to your affiliate offers is essential for earning commissions.

However, generating quality traffic can be a challenge. Invest in multiple traffic generation strategies such as search engine optimization (SEO), content marketing, social media marketing, email marketing, paid advertising, and influencer partnerships. Test and refine your strategies to find what works best for your niche and audience. Focus on attracting targeted traffic that is more likely to convert into sales.

4. Building Credibility and Trust: Affiliate marketing relies heavily on building trust with your audience. If your audience doesn't trust you, they are less likely to follow your recommendations or purchase through your affiliate links. To establish credibility, provide honest and valuable information about the products or services you promote. Avoid promoting products solely for the sake of earning a commission. Be transparent about your affiliations and disclose your relationship with the products or companies you endorse. Share personal experiences and testimonials to build trust with your audience.

5. Managing Affiliate Networks: Working with multiple affiliate networks or programs can be overwhelming. Keeping track of different platforms, payment schedules, and commission structures can become a challenge. Create a system to organize your affiliate partnerships, such as using spreadsheets or project management

tools. Stay updated on the latest offers and promotions from your affiliate networks. Monitor your affiliate links and ensure they are functioning correctly. Regularly review your performance metrics to identify which networks or programs are delivering the best results.

6. Adapting to Industry Changes: The digital marketing landscape is constantly evolving, and affiliate marketers need to adapt to industry changes. Stay updated on industry news, trends, and changes in algorithms or policies that may affect your marketing strategies. Continuously educate yourself through online courses, webinars, forums, and industry events. Be flexible and open to trying new approaches and techniques to stay ahead of the competition.

7. Compliance and Legal Issues: Compliance with advertising laws and regulations is crucial in affiliate marketing. Each country may have different rules regarding disclosure, data privacy, and promotional practices. Familiarize yourself with the regulations in your target markets and ensure your marketing campaigns comply with these guidelines. Clearly disclose your affiliate relationships to your audience, and ensure you handle and protect customer data in accordance with applicable laws, such as GDPR or CCPA.

Overcoming these challenges requires persistence,

continuous learning, and adapting to the ever-changing digital landscape. By focusing on providing value, building trust, and staying informed, affiliate marketers can increase their chances of success in this competitive field.

Dealing with competition and market saturation

As an affiliate marketer, competition and market saturation are common challenges you may face. Market saturation refers to a situation where there are already a significant number of affiliate marketers promoting the same products or services within a particular niche. Dealing with competition and market saturation requires a comprehensive approach involving strategic planning, differentiation, and continuous adaptation. Here's a step-by-step explanation:

1. Research and Select a Niche: Start by researching different niches to find one that aligns with your interests, expertise, and has the potential for profitability. Look for areas where there is still room for growth and where you can carve out a unique position.

2. Identify Your Target Audience: Once you've chosen a

niche, define your target audience. Understand their needs, preferences, and pain points. This will help you tailor your marketing efforts and differentiate yourself from competitors.

3. Competitor Analysis: Analyze your competition within your chosen niche. Identify the top affiliate marketers and study their strategies. Look for gaps and opportunities that they may have missed. This analysis will give you insights into what is working in the market and help you identify areas where you can differentiate yourself.

4. Develop a Unique Selling Proposition (USP): Differentiation is crucial in a saturated market. Determine your USP—what sets you apart from your competitors. It could be offering additional value, providing exceptional customer service, focusing on a specific sub-niche, or having exclusive partnerships. Highlight your USP in your marketing messages to attract and retain customers.

5. Build an Authority Brand: Establish yourself as an authority in your niche. Create high-quality content such as blog posts, videos, podcasts, or social media posts that provide value to your audience. Share your expertise, insights, and opinions to build trust and credibility. Leverage your unique perspective and voice

to stand out from the competition.

6. Diversify Traffic Sources: Relying on a single traffic source can be risky. Explore multiple channels to attract visitors to your affiliate offers. This could include search engine optimization (SEO), social media marketing, content marketing, email marketing, paid advertising, or collaborations with other influencers. Diversifying your traffic sources helps mitigate the impact of changes in algorithms or ad policies.

7. Continuous Learning and Adaptation: The digital marketing landscape is ever-evolving. Stay updated with the latest trends, technologies, and strategies. Monitor your competition and be willing to adapt your approach when necessary. Embrace new platforms and techniques to reach your target audience effectively.

8. Build Relationships with Affiliate Managers: Cultivate relationships with affiliate managers of the products or services you promote. They can provide insights, exclusive offers, and support, giving you an advantage over other affiliates. Building strong relationships may lead to preferential treatment, increased commissions, and access to valuable resources.

9. Test and Optimize: Continuously test different strategies, offers, and marketing techniques to identify what works best for your audience. Monitor key metrics

like conversion rates, click-through rates, and average order value. Use this data to optimize your campaigns, focusing on the most effective tactics.

10. Provide Exceptional Customer Experience: Deliver an outstanding customer experience to differentiate yourself. Respond promptly to customer queries, provide useful information, and ensure a seamless purchasing process. By going above and beyond, you can generate positive reviews, testimonials, and word-of-mouth referrals that help you stand out in a saturated market.

Remember, competition and market saturation are inevitable in any successful industry. However, by following these steps and continuously refining your strategies, you can position yourself as a trusted affiliate marketer and thrive amidst the competition.

Staying motivated and maintaining a long-term vision

Staying motivated and maintaining a long-term vision as an affiliate marketer can be challenging, but it is essential for your success in the field. Here is a comprehensive explanation of how you can stay motivated and maintain a long-term vision as an affiliate marketer:

1. Develop a Long-Term Vision: Beyond short-term goals, it's crucial to have a long-term vision for your affiliate marketing business. Visualize where you want to see yourself in the next few years and the kind of success you aim to achieve. Having a compelling vision will help you stay motivated during challenging times and keep your focus on the bigger picture.

2. Find Your Passion: Choose affiliate marketing niches that align with your interests and passions. When you are passionate about the products or services you promote, it becomes easier to stay motivated. Your enthusiasm will shine through in your content and marketing efforts, attracting and engaging your audience effectively.

3. Continuously Educate Yourself: Stay updated with the latest trends, strategies, and technologies in affiliate marketing. Attend webinars, read industry blogs, join relevant forums, and invest in courses or training programs. Expanding your knowledge and skills not only keeps you motivated but also allows you to adapt to the ever-changing landscape of affiliate marketing.

4. Surround Yourself with Positive Influences: Connect with like-minded individuals who share your goals and aspirations. Engage in affiliate marketing communities, join mastermind groups, or attend industry events. Surrounding yourself with positive and supportive people can help you stay motivated, exchange ideas, and learn from others' experiences.

5. Track Your Progress: Regularly track and measure your progress to see how far you've come. Celebrate your successes, no matter how small, and use them as motivation to keep moving forward. Additionally, identify areas where you may need improvement and set strategies to overcome challenges. The sense of accomplishment will boost your motivation and help you stay focused on your long-term vision.

6. Break Down Tasks and Prioritize: Affiliate marketing involves various tasks, such as content creation, SEO optimization, social media management, and relationship building. Break down these tasks into smaller, manageable steps, and prioritize them based on their importance and impact on your long-term goals. By focusing on one task at a time and making progress, you'll stay motivated and avoid feeling overwhelmed.

7. Reward Yourself: Set up a system of rewards for achieving milestones or completing challenging tasks.

Treat yourself to something you enjoy when you accomplish a goal or reach a specific target. The rewards will provide you with a sense of achievement and motivation to keep pushing forward.

8. Stay Positive and Practice Self-Care: Maintain a positive mindset and practice self-care. Affiliate marketing can have its ups and downs, and it's essential to stay resilient during setbacks. Take breaks, exercise, practice mindfulness, and engage in activities that rejuvenate you. By taking care of your physical and mental well-being, you'll maintain the motivation and focus needed for long-term success.

9. Adapt and Evolve: The affiliate marketing landscape is continually evolving, so it's crucial to adapt and embrace changes. Stay open to new opportunities, test different strategies, and be willing to learn from both successes and failures. Embracing change and innovation will keep your affiliate marketing business relevant and motivate you to keep growing.

Remember, staying motivated and maintaining a long-term vision as an affiliate marketer requires dedication, perseverance, and continuous effort. By following these strategies and staying focused on your goals, you'll increase your chances of long-term success in the affiliate marketing industry.

CONCLUSION

Recap of key concepts and strategies discussed throughout the book

Affiliate marketing is a popular online business model where affiliates promote products or services of other companies and earn a commission for each sale or lead they generate. Throughout the book, several key concepts and strategies are discussed to help you succeed in affiliate marketing. Here is a comprehensive recap:

1. Choosing the Right Niche: Select a niche that aligns with your interests, expertise, and market demand. Conduct thorough research to identify profitable niches with potential customers who are willing to spend money.

2. Building an Authority Website: Create a professional website or blog focused on your chosen niche. Provide valuable content, product reviews, and information that

engage your audience and establishes you as an authority in your niche.

3. Understanding Your Audience: Conduct market research to understand your target audience's needs, preferences, and pain points. Tailor your content and promotions to address their specific challenges and offer solutions that resonate with them.

4. Selecting Affiliate Programs: Choose reputable affiliate programs or networks that offer products or services related to your niche. Look for programs that provide competitive commissions, quality products, reliable tracking systems, and supportive affiliate managers.

5. Promoting Quality Products: Only promote products or services that you genuinely believe in and that offer value to your audience. Recommending subpar or low-quality products can damage your reputation and trust with your audience.

6. Content Marketing: Create high-quality, informative, and engaging content that attracts and retains your audience. Use various formats such as blog posts, videos, podcasts, and social media to diversify your content and reach a wider audience.

7. SEO Optimization: Implement search engine

optimization techniques to improve your website's visibility in search engine results. Conduct keyword research, optimize your content with relevant keywords, build high-quality backlinks, and ensure your site's technical aspects are optimized.

8. Email Marketing: Build an email list by offering valuable incentives, such as free e-books or exclusive content, in exchange for your audience's email addresses. Use email marketing campaigns to nurture relationships, provide value, and promote relevant affiliate products.

9. Social Media Marketing: Leverage social media platforms to promote your content, engage with your audience, and drive traffic to your website. Build a strong social media presence by sharing valuable content, participating in relevant communities, and leveraging influencer partnerships.

10. Paid Advertising: Consider using paid advertising channels such as Google Ads, Facebook Ads, or native advertising to drive targeted traffic to your website. Carefully monitor and optimize your campaigns to ensure a positive return on investment.

11. Tracking and Analytics: Use tracking tools and analytics platforms to monitor your affiliate marketing performance. Track clicks, conversions, and revenue

generated by each affiliate promotion to identify what works best and optimize your strategies accordingly.

12. Building Relationships: Foster relationships with your audience, fellow affiliates, and affiliate managers. Engage with your audience through comments, emails, and social media. Collaborate with other affiliates and share insights and strategies. Build rapport with affiliate managers to access exclusive promotions or negotiate higher commissions.

13. Continuous Learning and Adaptation: Stay updated with the latest trends, tools, and techniques in affiliate marketing. Attend industry conferences, join relevant forums and communities, and invest in educational resources to continually improve your skills and adapt to the evolving landscape.

Remember, success in affiliate marketing requires patience, persistence, and a focus on providing value to your audience. By implementing these key concepts and strategies, you can increase your chances of building a profitable affiliate marketing business.

Encouragement to take action and implement the

affiliate marketing blueprint

I'm glad to hear that you're interested in implementing an affiliate marketing blueprint! Taking action and pursuing your goals is an important step towards success. Here's some encouragement and guidance to help you get started:

1. Believe in yourself: Remember that you have the potential to achieve great things. Believe in your abilities and trust that you can learn and grow through the process of implementing the affiliate marketing blueprint.

2. Set clear goals: Define your goals and objectives for your affiliate marketing venture. Whether it's earning a specific income, reaching a certain audience, or promoting products you're passionate about, having clear goals will give you direction and motivation.

3. Educate yourself: Invest time in learning about affiliate marketing strategies, best practices, and the latest industry trends. There are numerous online resources, courses, and communities that can provide valuable insights and guidance. Equip yourself with knowledge to make informed decisions.

4. Start small, but start now: Don't wait for the perfect

moment or until you have all the answers. Begin by taking small steps towards implementing your affiliate marketing blueprint. Start building your website or blog, research potential affiliate programs, and create engaging content. The important thing is to take action and get started.

5. Stay consistent: Consistency is key in affiliate marketing. Set a regular schedule for creating and promoting content, engaging with your audience, and tracking your progress. Consistent effort over time will yield better results than sporadic bursts of activity.

6. Be patient and persistent: Affiliate marketing is not an overnight success story. It takes time to build an audience, establish relationships with affiliate partners, and generate substantial income. Be patient with yourself and the process, and stay persistent even when facing challenges or setbacks.

7. Learn from your experiences: As you implement your affiliate marketing blueprint, you'll encounter both successes and failures. Embrace them as opportunities for growth and learning. Analyze what works and what doesn't, and adjust your strategies accordingly. The more you learn from your experiences, the better you'll become at affiliate marketing.

8. Stay motivated and positive: Affiliate marketing can

be a journey with ups and downs. Surround yourself with positive influences, connect with like-minded individuals, and celebrate your milestones along the way. Maintain a positive mindset, and let your passion and enthusiasm for your chosen niche drive you forward.

Remember, taking action is the first step towards turning your affiliate marketing blueprint into a reality. Believe in yourself, stay committed, and never stop learning. Best of luck on your affiliate marketing journey!

ABOUT THE AUTHOR

Solomon is a renowned expert in the field of affiliate marketing. With years of experience and a deep understanding of the industry, Solomon has established him selves as a trusted authority on the subject.

Solomon has helped countless individuals and businesses achieve success in affiliate marketing. Solomon as a remarkable ability to break down complex concepts into easy-to-understand terms, making his book accessible to beginners while also offering valuable strategies for seasoned marketers.

Solomon journey in affiliate marketing began years ago when he recognized the tremendous potential of this business model. He immersed selves in the world of digital marketing, honing his skills through trial and error, experimenting with different strategies, and closely studying successful affiliate marketers. His dedication and perseverance led to significant achievements, which propelled him to share his expertise through writing.

In "Affiliate Marketing Blueprint," Solomon provides readers with a comprehensive guide to building a successful affiliate marketing business from scratch. The book covers everything from understanding the fundamentals of affiliate marketing to advanced techniques for maximizing earnings. With a step-by-step approach, Solomon outlines proven strategies, industry secrets, and practical tips to help readers create a profitable affiliate marketing venture.

Solomon is committed to helping aspiring affiliate marketers by providing ongoing support and sharing the latest trends and strategies in the field. His dedication to the success of others has earned him a loyal following and solidified his reputation as a trusted mentor.

www.ingramcontent.com/pod-product-compliance
Lightning Source LLC
Chambersburg PA
CBHW072028230526
45466CB00020B/1112